Copyright © 2024 Andrea Oliver

All rights reserved

The characters and events portrayed in this book are fictitious. Any similarity to real persons, living or dead, is coincidental and not intended by the author.

No part of this book may be reproduced, or stored in a retrieval system, or transmitted in any form or by any means, electronic, mechanical, photocopying, recording, or otherwise, without express written permission of the publisher.

Cover design by: Art Painter
Library of Congress Control Number: 2018675309
Printed in the United States of America

CONTENTS

Copyright
Introduction — 2
Chapter 1: What Makes an Opportunity Global? — 6
Chapter 2: Economic Indicators and — 11
Chapter 3: The Pillars of a Global Gold Rush — 17
Chapter 4: Navigating Cultural and Economic Barriers — 23
Chapter 5: The Power of Localization — 29
Chapter 6: Identifying the Infrastructure — 35
Chapter 7: Building an Entry Strategy — 43
Chapter 8: Leveraging Local Partnerships and Networks — 49
Chapter 9: Funding Your International Expansion — 55
Chapter 10: Scaling Successfully Across Borders — 62
Chapter 11: Staying Agile in a Rapidly Changing World — 69
Chapter 12: Creating a Long-Term Vision for International Growth — 76
Chapter 13: Case Study — Fintech in Africa — 84
Chapter 14: Case Study — Renewable Energy in Developing Nations — 91
Conclusion: Becoming a Global Gold Rush Visionary — 99
Appendix — 102

ANDREA OLIVER

Global Gold Rush:
Spotting and Seizing Opportunities
in International Markets

INTRODUCTION

Welcome to the world of global entrepreneurship, where borders are more like suggestions and opportunities are as plentiful as coffee shops in Seattle. Today, "going global" isn't just a buzzword; it's the secret ingredient in the recipe for success. In a world as connected as ours, the potential to tap into new markets, explore emerging technologies, and meet the needs of underserved populations is simply too good to pass up.

Gone are the days when expanding your business meant sending a ship full of cargo and hoping it didn't sink. These days, you can sell a product to someone halfway across the world with a click, and thanks to high-speed internet and digital platforms, you can have customers from Cairo to Calgary without ever leaving your desk.

So, why go global? Simple: because the world is full of untapped potential. While your home market may be cozy and familiar, there's a big wide world out there full of growing economies and tech-hungry consumers just waiting for something new to hit their shores. In other words, there's gold in them hills—if you're willing to look beyond your backyard.

Why Go Global?

Let's talk about the benefits of thinking beyond your local market. Expanding globally isn't just about adding some fancy locations to your business card; it's about accessing growing economies, connecting with underserved populations, and hopping on the latest in emerging tech before anyone else gets to it. It's about finding that sweet spot where demand is high, competition is low, and growth is ripe for the taking.

Consider this: some of the fastest-growing economies in the world are outside the traditional Western markets. Places like Southeast Asia, parts of Africa, and South America are seeing booming demand for everything from consumer goods to clean energy, thanks to a rapidly expanding middle class. These areas are primed for innovation, and the first to enter with a solid offering could see the kind of growth that makes traditional markets look like yesterday's news.

And don't even get me started on emerging technologies. From fintech revolutions in Africa to clean energy in Latin America, markets worldwide are welcoming innovation with open arms. By stepping into these spaces, you're not just growing your customer base—you're helping to shape the future of industries and the economy itself. Plus, being the "new kid on the block" comes with a level of excitement and intrigue that can work wonders for brand loyalty. When you're first to market, customers see you not just as another company, but as a pioneer.

Revisiting the Gold Rush Model for a Global Landscape

You've heard of the Gold Rush, right? Men and women rushing west with dreams of finding gold and striking it rich. Now, fast-forward to today, and that spirit of adventure is very much alive—except now the gold isn't buried in California streams; it's hiding in international markets, just waiting for someone savvy enough to dig it out. Think of going global as your own modern-day Gold Rush, where the "gold" isn't literal nuggets but untapped opportunities, underserved markets, and a customer base you didn't even know you needed.

Just like the prospectors of old, today's global entrepreneurs know that the best time to jump in is before the market gets crowded. The early movers in today's global landscape have a distinct advantage. They get to set up shop before the market is saturated, establish relationships with local suppliers, and build brand loyalty in a way that's tough for latecomers to replicate.

So how do you spot your own Gold Rush opportunity? It's about recognizing where demand is growing faster than supply, understanding the unique needs of each region, and figuring out how to deliver a product or service that genuinely makes a difference. This isn't about blindly throwing darts at a map; it's about smart, calculated moves that take into account everything from local culture to economic trends. When done right, you're not just entering a new market—you're creating a legacy that could transform industries and change lives.

In this book, we'll look at exactly how to identify, evaluate, and capitalize on global opportunities, using the Gold Rush model as a framework. We'll break down how to know when to jump in, how to scale when the time is right, and, most importantly, how to hold your ground when everyone around you thinks you're a little bit crazy for "going global."

So buckle up—your Gold Rush awaits, and this time, the stakes are higher, the opportunities are richer, and the world is yours for the taking.

ANDREA OLIVER

Part I: Understanding Global Gold Rush Patterns

CHAPTER 1: WHAT MAKES AN OPPORTUNITY GLOBAL?

Alright, so you're pumped to go global. You've got your metaphorical pickaxe and shovel, and you're ready to find your own slice of international gold. But before you set off digging, let's talk about what really makes an opportunity "global." Spoiler alert: it's not just a product or service you can sell anywhere. A true global opportunity is one that taps into demand that knows no borders, meets needs that transcend cultures, and rides the wave of technology and connectivity that's making the world feel more like a village than a patchwork of isolated markets.

In this chapter, we're going to break down the elements that turn a local win into a global jackpot, show you how global demand, tech, and connectivity are reshaping what qualifies as a "Gold Rush," and dig into the key differences between local and global goldmines. Let's go.

The New Frontier: Demand That Knows No Borders

The first hallmark of a global opportunity? Demand that travels well. Think about it: coffee, smartphones, streaming services—these are things people want everywhere, not just in your hometown. The best global opportunities are the ones that cater to universal needs or desires. They solve a problem, scratch an itch, or offer something that almost anyone, anywhere, would want. This doesn't mean every product should be one-size-fits-all, but it does mean that the core appeal has to resonate across cultures.

Take fintech, for instance. Access to financial services is a universal need. In Africa, mobile money platforms are helping millions manage their finances in areas where banks are scarce. In Asia, digital wallets have turned into super apps that let users shop, pay bills, and even book travel. The details may vary, but the need for accessible financial tools? It's the same everywhere.

Lesson Learned: Look for demand that isn't constrained by borders. If your offering makes life easier, faster, or more fun in a way that resonates globally, you might be onto something big.

Technology: The Game-Changer of Global Reach

Global opportunities are a lot easier to seize these days, thanks to technology. Gone are the days when expanding meant setting up costly storefronts in far-off countries. With the internet, social media, and digital marketing, you can test the waters in multiple countries without leaving your desk. Today, technology allows businesses to scale across borders at a fraction of the cost and time it used to take. And with tech comes data—loads of it. You can track who's interested in your product, how they're interacting with it, and which parts of your offering resonate best, no matter where they're located.

Tech isn't just making it easier to expand; it's also creating entirely new categories of demand. Consider streaming services. A decade ago, the idea of watching the latest Hollywood movie or South Korean drama on your phone from anywhere in the world sounded like science fiction. Now it's everyday reality. The demand for digital content is a direct result of better internet infrastructure and affordable mobile devices, turning content into a global product with sky-high demand.

Lesson Learned: Technology isn't just a tool; it's a launching pad. If your product or service leverages tech to reach people globally, you've got a head start in turning local demand into international opportunity.

Connectivity: The Glue That Binds the Global Market

Demand and tech are great, but without connectivity, they're like an engine without fuel. Connectivity—think social media, high-speed internet, and e-commerce platforms—is what turns an idea with international potential into a global powerhouse. It's the network that lets you sell to someone in Mumbai from your office in Miami or ship a product from Manila to Milan. Connectivity also means information flows fast, so people everywhere can see, hear about, and learn to love your product at the same time.

This connectivity gives global opportunities an urgency and visibility that local markets can't match. People in different parts of the world are increasingly sharing experiences, styles, and ideas, which means the gap between "local" and "global" tastes is shrinking. If you can tap into that shared culture—whether it's through fashion, tech, or even food—you're looking at a global Gold Rush opportunity.

Lesson Learned: Connectivity turns global dreams into reality. If you can connect your product to the world, you can connect it to a customer base far larger than you ever thought possible.

Local vs. Global Gold Rushes: What's the Difference?

Now, let's talk about the key differences between striking gold in a local market versus finding it on the global stage. Both types of opportunities are exciting, but they come with different challenges and rewards.

1. Scalability and Reach

A local Gold Rush is like finding a vein of gold in your backyard. You mine it, you sell it, you make a tidy profit—but your reach is naturally limited. A global Gold Rush, on the other hand, is like stumbling upon a massive deposit that stretches across continents. You can keep mining, scaling, and reaching more people, which means there's room for exponentially greater growth.

2. Market Dynamics

Local markets often follow their own patterns, influenced by regional culture, economics, and consumer habits. A global market, however, requires a balance between understanding universal appeal and tailoring for local nuances. You'll need to do your homework on cultural expectations, buying power, and even things like regulatory quirks to thrive globally.

3. Risk and Reward

Going global brings bigger risks along with bigger rewards. In a local market, your exposure is limited; if something goes wrong, you can often pivot quickly. But in a global market, the stakes are higher. Fluctuations in currency, changes in political stability, or shifts in regulatory policy in just one of your target markets can have ripple effects. The upside? Get it right, and you're looking at growth, revenue, and brand recognition on a scale that's nearly impossible to achieve locally.

Lesson Learned: The global Gold Rush is bigger, bolder, and riskier, but the payoff can be game-changing. It's not for the faint of heart, but then again, neither is finding gold.

Final Thoughts: Mining for Global Gold

What makes an opportunity global? It's about demand that knows no borders, technology that lets you scale, and connectivity that allows you to reach a diverse audience from anywhere. It's about thinking big, taking calculated risks, and having the flexibility to adapt as you go. The key to finding your Gold Rush isn't about stumbling upon a lucky strike—it's about seeing the potential in a world that's more interconnected than ever before.

In the coming chapters, we'll dive deeper into identifying these opportunities, understanding how to approach new markets, and making your mark in a world that's ripe for the next Gold Rush.

CHAPTER 2: ECONOMIC INDICATORS AND

Global Trends to Watch

If you're after global gold, you'll need a compass to point you in the right direction. Fortunately, in today's world, you don't have to stumble around blindly in search of opportunity. The modern prospector's map is packed with economic indicators, trends, and patterns that signal where the next big Gold Rush might be. Think of GDP growth, shifts in consumer behavior, and policy changes as the glittering signs that show where things are heating up.

In this chapter, we'll dive into these key indicators and trends across industries like tech, sustainability, and healthcare to help you spot where demand is heading before it arrives. Knowing what to look for is the first step in striking it big—so let's sharpen those skills and get ready to read the signs.

Follow the Growth: GDP and Economic Expansion

First up, let's talk GDP—Gross Domestic Product. While it might sound like economic jargon, GDP is actually your best friend when scouting for global opportunities. It's a measure of a country's total economic output, and a rising GDP is one of the strongest signs of a healthy, growing economy. When a nation's GDP is climbing, it usually means businesses are flourishing, consumers are spending, and there's room for new products and services to capture a slice of the action.

But don't just look at the GDP growth itself; dig a little deeper. Check out what's driving that growth. Is it fueled by an increase in manufacturing, tech development, or consumer spending? Each growth driver points to different types of demand, and knowing where that demand is concentrated can help you target your approach.

For instance, Southeast Asia has been a hotspot of growth for years, with GDP increases driven by a burgeoning middle class and tech investment. China and India? Powerhouses in manufacturing and tech development. Latin America is seeing growth in agriculture and consumer goods. Each region has its own flavor of opportunity—and GDP is often the first clue.

Lesson Learned: Rising GDP is your neon sign for opportunity, but look beyond the numbers to understand what's fueling that growth.

Consumer Behavior Shifts: The Pulse of the Market

If GDP is the sign that a market is healthy, consumer behavior is the heartbeat that tells you what people actually want. And these days, tracking behavior is as easy as looking at social media trends, e-commerce patterns, and even the latest apps people are downloading. In an age where consumers are constantly sharing what they like (or dislike), businesses have a direct line to what's hot—and what's not.

Keep an eye on shifts like a growing appetite for luxury goods, a turn toward health and wellness products, or a surge in e-commerce spending. Consumer behavior can also reveal new needs in specific regions, like a demand for digital payments in Africa or sustainable fashion in Europe. Knowing where these shifts are happening is invaluable, and the sooner you catch wind of these changes, the sooner you can align your offerings.

- **Example**: Take the rapid rise in demand for plant-based foods, spurred by consumers' growing interest in health and environmental sustainability. Companies like Beyond Meat and Oatly didn't just create products—they tapped into a consumer shift, expanding quickly into global markets hungry for healthy and ethical options.

Lesson Learned: Consumer behavior shifts tell you what people care about and, more importantly, what they're willing to spend on. Follow these trends to find out where demand is growing.

Policy Changes: Government as Your Hidden Partner

Believe it or not, policy changes can be your best friend in the hunt for new markets. Governments around the world use policy to shape everything from consumer protection laws to environmental standards. When you spot a government leaning heavily into renewable energy, tech investment, or healthcare reform, take note—it means they're putting resources and support behind these areas, creating a fertile ground for businesses to thrive.

Countries often encourage foreign businesses through tax incentives, grants, or easier regulations for industries they want to grow. For example, renewable energy is a sector seeing massive government support worldwide, with policy changes aimed at reducing carbon footprints. If you're in clean energy, sustainable agriculture, or green tech, pay close attention to government initiatives—they can make or break the ease of doing business.

- **Example**: In India, government policies encouraging digital payments and e-commerce have made the country a hotbed for fintech and online retail. Companies like Amazon and Flipkart thrived here by aligning with these policy-driven incentives, which reduced barriers to digital commerce and drew millions of new users online.

Lesson Learned: Government policies can create or close doors. Know what governments are prioritizing, and you'll know where business is likely to thrive.

Global Trends Worth Watching

In the search for global gold, some trends are more than just passing fads—they're tectonic shifts that are transforming industries, economies, and the way we live. Here are a few big ones driving demand and shaping the global marketplace.

1. Technology and Digital Transformation

Let's be real: technology is no longer just a sector; it's a backbone of almost every industry out there. From artificial intelligence (AI) and the Internet of Things (IoT) to fintech and cloud computing, digital transformation is sweeping the globe, creating demand for products and services that didn't even exist a decade ago. And it's not just limited to the tech-savvy—every business, from a small shop in Vietnam to a manufacturing plant in Brazil, is looking for ways to get digital.

Opportunities in tech aren't limited to software. Hardware, cybersecurity, digital infrastructure, and training are all growing markets. If you're in tech, pay attention to the regions embracing it the fastest and the industries ripe for a digital upgrade.

- **Example**: Southeast Asia has seen an explosion in e-commerce, driven by growing smartphone use and improved internet access. Companies like Shopee and Lazada have capitalized on this digital transformation by building e-commerce ecosystems that connect millions of customers with sellers across borders.

Lesson Learned: Digital transformation is creating waves across industries. If you can make tech accessible, affordable, or more efficient, you're sitting on a goldmine.

2. Sustainability and Green Innovation

If tech is the brain of global growth, sustainability is the conscience. Consumers and governments alike are leaning into greener choices, demanding eco-friendly products, renewable energy, and sustainable practices. This trend isn't just a phase—it's the future. And businesses that can get ahead of it will find themselves with a long-term edge.

Clean energy, electric vehicles, sustainable packaging, and even eco-tourism are all industries poised for rapid growth. If your product or service can reduce waste, cut emissions, or offer a cleaner alternative, you're not just joining a market trend—you're becoming part of a global movement.

- **Example**: Tesla's early focus on electric vehicles didn't just create a new market; it helped shift the entire automotive industry. Today, Tesla's influence is felt worldwide as governments push for lower emissions and consumers increasingly seek greener transport options.

Lesson Learned: Sustainability isn't just a checkbox—it's a demand. Green innovation is here to stay, and there's a lot of room for businesses that can deliver eco-friendly solutions.

3. Healthcare and Wellbeing

Healthcare is going global, and as populations grow and age, demand for healthcare products, services, and technology is skyrocketing. Whether it's telemedicine in remote areas, wearable health devices, or mental wellness apps, health and wellness is a booming sector with endless opportunities.

The pandemic showed us that healthcare needs are universal, and the shift toward preventive care, digital health solutions, and mental health awareness is only intensifying. If you have a product or service that promotes wellbeing, improves healthcare access, or supports healthier lifestyles, you're in a space with nearly limitless growth potential.

- **Example**: Telehealth companies like Babylon Health have expanded internationally by offering healthcare access to underserved communities. The success of telemedicine during the pandemic showed that demand for remote healthcare options isn't going away—it's only growing.

Lesson Learned: Healthcare is the gift that keeps on giving (in business terms, anyway). If your product improves lives or makes healthcare more accessible, the world's your oyster.

Final Thoughts: Reading the Signs of Global Opportunity

Identifying a global Gold Rush isn't about having a crystal ball—it's about knowing where to look. Economic indicators like GDP growth, shifts in consumer behavior, and changes in government policy are the building blocks of a booming market. And when you pair those with major trends in technology, sustainability, and healthcare, you're not just finding opportunities—you're spotting the future.

The best part? These trends are only accelerating. As global connectivity strengthens, demand for tech, green solutions, and healthcare is only going to grow. So, pay attention to these signs, watch the trends, and get ready to seize the opportunities as they arise. The world is full of gold—if you know where to dig.

CHAPTER 3: THE PILLARS OF A GLOBAL GOLD RUSH

Welcome to the fundamentals of finding gold on a global scale. By now, we've looked at the economic indicators and trends that point to the next big opportunity. But what about the characteristics that separate successful international ventures from the ones that fizzle out? The answer lies in three core pillars: scalability, adaptability, and local relevance. These are the hallmarks of ventures that manage to thrive across borders, cultures, and economic climates. When you build a business around these pillars, you're not just finding a Gold Rush; you're creating a blueprint for success.

In this chapter, we'll dive into these pillars and look at real-life examples—case studies that show how they work in action, from the smartphone revolution in Asia to the fintech boom in Africa and clean energy growth in Europe. So, grab your pickaxe and let's get into the nuts and bolts of building a global empire.

Pillar 1: Scalability—Building for the Long Haul

First up: scalability. If your business isn't scalable, it's like building a sandcastle on a windy beach. It might look great, but it won't last long. Scalability is the ability to grow without needing to reinvent the wheel every time you enter a new market. A scalable business model adapts to larger demands and operates across multiple regions without losing quality or racking up massive costs. It's about creating a foundation that can support growth instead of crumbling under it.

One of the best examples? The smartphone revolution in Asia. When smartphone manufacturers entered the Asian market, they weren't just selling fancy gadgets—they were offering a scalable solution to communication and connectivity. Companies like Xiaomi figured out how to deliver affordable, quality smartphones to a massive population. By optimizing production, streamlining distribution, and embracing e-commerce, they could scale quickly, offering the right products at the right price.

- **Case Study: Xiaomi's Smartphone Strategy in Asia**
  Xiaomi's approach was simple yet powerful: build high-quality smartphones with just enough features to satisfy customers, without the extra frills that drive up costs. By focusing on value for money, Xiaomi could reach a huge customer base across Asia, capturing the attention of first-time smartphone users. This strategy made Xiaomi a leader in markets like India, proving that scalability isn't about building the flashiest product—it's about delivering exactly what people need in a way that's easy to replicate and expand.

Lesson Learned: A scalable model keeps things efficient and cost-effective. When your product or service can be easily adapted to growing demand, you're set up for success.

Pillar 2: Adaptability—When Flexibility Is Your Best Friend

Next is adaptability—the ability to pivot, tweak, and adjust as you go. In global markets, adaptability is your safety net, helping you weather unexpected challenges like regulatory changes, cultural differences, or shifting consumer expectations. A rigid business model might work locally, but on the global stage, it's adaptability that keeps you in the game.

Nowhere is this clearer than in the rise of fintech in Africa. Traditional banks were slow to reach rural areas, and millions of people had no access to basic financial services. Fintech companies spotted this gap and created a way to offer banking without brick-and-mortar locations. Mobile money platforms like M-Pesa in Kenya adapted to the local context, providing banking through mobile phones, often without the need for a bank account or even internet access.

- **Case Study: M-Pesa's Fintech Success in Africa**
  M-Pesa adapted to the unique needs of African consumers by turning basic mobile phones into financial lifelines. They didn't just replicate Western banking models; they created a whole new category of banking that worked in areas with limited infrastructure. M-Pesa's flexibility allowed them to expand rapidly and reach millions, proving that the ability to adapt isn't just a nice-to-have—it's essential for success in challenging markets.

Lesson Learned: Adaptability means listening to the market and meeting people where they are. When you build flexibility into your approach, you can make the most of any market, no matter how different it is from your own.

Pillar 3: Local Relevance—Becoming a Household Name

Finally, we have local relevance. This is where a global Gold Rush either succeeds or falls flat. Just because something worked in one country doesn't mean it will resonate everywhere. To win hearts (and wallets) in new markets, you have to make your product feel relevant to local consumers. This means understanding their needs, respecting their culture, and often tweaking your product or message to fit the local vibe.

Look no further than the clean energy revolution in Europe for a perfect example of local relevance. European consumers and governments have long supported environmental initiatives, and their demand for clean energy is high. Solar and wind power companies recognized this, and by aligning their offerings with the public's values, they turned renewable energy into a mainstream choice.

- **Case Study: Ørsted's Clean Energy Transition in Europe**
  Danish energy company Ørsted started as a fossil fuel giant but transformed itself into a leader in renewable energy by focusing on offshore wind power, especially in Europe. Ørsted's shift wasn't just about supplying energy; it was about becoming part of the broader European movement toward sustainability. The company embraced the values of local consumers, aligning its mission with the environmental priorities of the region. As a result, Ørsted now powers millions of homes with wind energy, demonstrating that local relevance can turn a company into a leader in its industry.

Lesson Learned: Local relevance is about more than just selling a product—it's about understanding the local culture, values, and priorities. When you make your offering relevant to the people, you become part of their world, not just another outsider trying to cash in.

The Power of These Pillars in Action

When you combine scalability, adaptability, and local relevance, you're setting yourself up for a business model that can weather just about anything. Look at how these pillars played out in each of our case studies:

1. **In Asia's smartphone boom, scalability allowed companies like Xiaomi to reach millions, delivering affordable, quality phones at a pace that kept up with demand.**
2. **In Africa's fintech revolution, adaptability enabled M-Pesa to meet the unique challenges of the market, reaching customers in places traditional banks**

couldn't.
3. **In Europe's clean energy push, local relevance helped Ørsted become a trusted provider by aligning with the values and priorities of European consumers.**

These aren't just isolated stories—they're blueprints for how you can approach your own global Gold Rush. By building on these pillars, you're not just increasing your chances of success; you're creating a foundation that can adapt, expand, and resonate no matter where you take it.

Final Thoughts: Your Own Global Gold Rush

These pillars aren't abstract theories; they're real-world strategies that have fueled some of the biggest global success stories. Scalability gives you the room to grow, adaptability keeps you resilient, and local relevance makes sure your product feels like it belongs. When you focus on these three pillars, you're not just preparing to enter new markets—you're preparing to thrive in them.

As we move forward, keep these pillars in mind. They're not only your guide to building a sustainable global business but also your map to striking gold wherever opportunity arises. The world is waiting, and if you're ready to build something scalable, adaptable, and relevant, you're more than ready to take on the global stage.

Part II: Spotting Global Opportunities

CHAPTER 4: NAVIGATING CULTURAL AND ECONOMIC BARRIERS

So you've found a promising market, set up your business, and now you're ready to make an impression. But before you go full steam ahead, there's a crucial checkpoint: understanding the cultural and economic landscape of the country you're entering. Because let's be honest—no one wants to be that foreign company stumbling into a new market, unaware of local norms, baffled by legal requirements, and delivering products that miss the mark.

Navigating cultural and economic barriers isn't just about "fitting in"; it's about building trust, staying compliant, and proving to your new customers that you understand them. In this chapter, we'll dive into the art of understanding local nuances, exploring how to align with economic realities and cultural expectations, and offering practical tips to ensure you're stepping into this new market with respect, relevance, and finesse.

Cracking the Code of Cultural Nuances

Every market has its unique cultural fingerprint, and even the subtlest details can make or break your success. Language, humor, social norms, and even colors can carry different meanings across cultures, and knowing these nuances is key to connecting with consumers on their level.

Take something as simple as color: In the United States, white is often associated with purity, while in many Asian cultures, it's linked to mourning. Or think about humor—what's funny in one country might fall flat or even offend in another. It's these little things that add up, shaping how your brand is perceived.

To get this right, start with research. Observe how local competitors communicate, what language they use, and the tone they adopt. Pay attention to cultural icons, symbols, and trends in the country you're entering. Better yet, talk to locals—get a feel for what they value, what they avoid, and what truly matters to them.

- **Example**: When Coca-Cola entered China, they faced a challenge in translating their name. Early translations led to names that sounded like "Bite the Wax Tadpole," a rather unfortunate mix-up! Eventually, Coca-Cola rebranded in Mandarin as "Kekou Kele," which translates to "Tasty Fun"—an instant hit.

Lesson Learned: Get a handle on the nuances. From language and color to humor and tone, understanding cultural cues ensures you're showing up as a brand that respects and celebrates the local context.

Economic Frameworks and Legal Essentials

Next up: the economics and legalities. Every country has its own set of regulations, tax structures, and economic frameworks. And while it might not be as thrilling as brainstorming a new marketing campaign, knowing these basics is crucial to keeping your business on solid ground.

1. **Regulatory Requirements**: Some countries have strict regulations for foreign companies, while others are more open. In some markets, you might need a local

partner or sponsor; in others, there are certain industries where foreign ownership is limited. Always check what's required and consult with local legal experts if needed.
2. **Taxes and Tariffs**: Don't let tax surprises catch you off guard. Many countries impose import taxes, value-added tax (VAT), or additional tariffs on foreign goods. Plan for these in your budget, as they can impact your pricing strategy. Consider consulting a local accountant who understands the specifics of cross-border business.
3. **Labor Laws**: If you're planning to hire locally, be aware of the labor laws. Minimum wages, work hours, benefits, and leave policies vary widely. Knowing these laws helps you stay compliant and ensures your local team is treated fairly.
- **Example**: Uber learned this the hard way when entering various international markets. In some regions, regulatory and labor laws clashed with their business model, requiring Uber to adapt operations, classify drivers as employees, or, in some cases, face legal battles.

Lesson Learned: Legal frameworks and economic conditions vary from place to place. Do your homework or get local advice to keep your business aligned and avoid unpleasant surprises.

Aligning with Consumer Expectations

Understanding the culture is one thing, but knowing what your consumers expect is another. Consumer expectations around quality, customer service, and pricing differ from market to market. What might seem like a luxury in one country could be a necessity in another—and vice versa.

- **Quality Standards**: For example, a higher level of quality might be expected in Japan, where consumers are known for their attention to detail, while in other mar-

kets, a lower-cost product may be more appealing.
- **Customer Service**: In some cultures, personalized, attentive service is highly valued, while in others, consumers prioritize speed and efficiency over personal interaction. Knowing these preferences allows you to shape your service approach accordingly.
- **Pricing Expectations**: Pricing isn't just a number; it's a reflection of perceived value. In countries where the economy is strong, consumers might be willing to pay more for premium products, while in emerging markets, a more affordable price could be the key to capturing attention.
- **Example**: IKEA learned about consumer expectations when they entered India. Initially, they offered flat-pack furniture, which was a hit globally but less popular in India, where many consumers are used to pre-assembled furniture. IKEA adapted, offering assembly services to meet this expectation and won the market's favor.

Lesson Learned: Look closely at what consumers expect in terms of quality, service, and price. Matching these expectations is your ticket to gaining loyalty and long-term growth.

Tips for Researching and Adapting to Local Values and Conditions

To truly make an impact in a new market, you need to go beyond assumptions and dive into real, ground-level research. Here are some proven ways to understand local values and align with the market's economic conditions.

1. Conduct Market Research with Local Insights

Go beyond the numbers and gather insights from local sources. Speak with consumers, observe local competitors, and use market research firms that specialize in the region. If you can, spend time on the ground (or, if that's not possible, work with local consultants). Look for what's missing in the market and see how you can fill that gap.

2. Partner with Local Experts

When in doubt, consult the pros. Partnering with local consultants, lawyers, or business advisors is one of the smartest moves you can make. They'll have the inside knowledge of regulations, consumer behavior, and culture that can be hard to find on your own. Plus, they'll help you sidestep common pitfalls that new market entrants often face.

- **Example**: Netflix partnered with local telecom providers in India to offer mobile-only plans. This adaptation came from local insights, recognizing that data usage is costly for many Indian consumers and that most use smartphones for streaming. By making Netflix more accessible, they gained a loyal user base.

3. Adjust Marketing to Speak to Local Values

The same marketing campaign that makes waves in New York might flop in Tokyo or Sao Paulo. Tailor your messaging to reflect local values, customs, and aspirations. This doesn't mean you have to reinvent your brand, but small tweaks can make a big difference. Think about what matters to your target audience and weave that into your campaign.

4. Adapt Your Product or Service Offerings

Sometimes, a little customization goes a long way. Consider whether there are ways to adapt your product or service to better suit the needs of the local market. This could mean adding new features, offering a different version of your product, or even rethinking your packaging.

- **Example**: McDonald's is famous for its ability to localize its menu. In India, where beef is off-limits for much of the population, McDonald's created a range of vegetarian options, including the McAloo Tikki Burger. By respecting local dietary customs, they earned a place in the market.

Lesson Learned: Tailoring your approach to meet local values and needs can be the difference between fitting in and standing out.

Final Thoughts: Navigating the Maze of Cultural and Economic Barriers

Expanding into new markets is an adventure, but it's not without its challenges. Cultural nuances, economic frameworks, and consumer expectations can feel like a maze to navigate, but with the right approach, you'll find your way through. Remember, each market is unique, and taking the time to respect and understand these differences is what separates the businesses that thrive from those that flounder.

By staying informed, working with local experts, and adapting your offerings to suit local needs, you're not just breaking down barriers—you're building bridges. And in the world of global entrepreneurship, that's what creates a lasting, loyal customer base.

So, as you embark on your international journey, remember: success isn't just about bringing a great product to market; it's about doing it in a way that resonates with, respects, and values the people who make up that market. With a little cultural sensitivity and a lot of curiosity, you'll be well on your way to becoming a global success.

CHAPTER 5: THE POWER OF LOCALIZATION

Congratulations! You've done your research, learned the lay of the land, and made sure your business is ready for international expansion. But now comes the big question: how do you make sure people actually *want* what you're offering? The answer lies in localization—adapting your product or service to fit the language, lifestyle, and buying habits of each region you enter.

Localization is more than a translation exercise or slapping your product into a new market with a "we're here!" banner. It's about becoming part of the community and delivering value in a way that resonates with local culture, norms, and everyday life. Done right, localization is one of the most powerful tools for turning a global idea into a local favorite. Let's dive into how to make this work—and look at a few companies that nailed it along the way.

Speaking the Language: More Than Just Translation

First things first: if your product isn't speaking the same language as your customers, you're already at a disadvantage. And we're not just talking about literal language (though that's a big part of it). Localization goes beyond swapping words; it means adopting the tone, slang, and expressions that truly connect with people in that region. The right language makes your product feel familiar, while the wrong one can make it feel like an outsider.

- **Example**: Airbnb understood this when expanding globally. Rather than simply translating its platform, Airbnb adapted its website to use local expressions and cultural references, creating a more comfortable experience for users. In Japan, for instance, they emphasized aspects of hospitality that resonate deeply with Japanese culture, such as respect for privacy and attention to detail.

Lesson Learned: Speak the local language in every sense of the word. Adapt your tone, phrasing, and even product descriptions to fit the region and make users feel at home.

Lifestyle Fit: Making Your Product Part of Everyday Life

Localization isn't just about what people see; it's also about how your product fits into their daily lives. Consider how people in a particular region might use your product differently than people at home. Lifestyle habits vary widely across the globe, and finding a way to adapt your offering to local routines and expectations can be the difference between standing out and blending in.

- **Example**: Netflix quickly learned this lesson when they expanded to India. Recognizing that many Indian consumers access the internet via mobile devices and prefer data-efficient options, they introduced a mobile-only plan. It allowed users to stream on their phones for a lower price, making Netflix a practical option in a region where mobile is king.

Lesson Learned: Adapt your product to fit into local routines and habits. When you understand how people live, you can adjust your offering to meet them where they're at.

Buying Habits: Pricing, Payments, and Purchase Pathways

Buying habits aren't just about whether people prefer online or in-store shopping. They include how people view pricing, payment options, and even the checkout experience. In some markets, people are comfortable paying online, while in others, cash-on-delivery (COD) is still king. Knowing these habits and aligning with them can make a world of difference.

- **Example**: Amazon understood this when entering India, where many consumers prefer COD due to limited credit card access. Rather than force a change in behavior, Amazon embraced COD and even invested in logistics to make it seamless. This adaptation was crucial to Amazon's success in India, making it one of the go-to platforms for online shopping.

Lesson Learned: Tailor your payment options and pricing to meet local expectations. If your purchase pathway feels natural to consumers, they'll feel more inclined to trust and use your platform.

Success Stories: Companies that Mastered Localization

Let's look at a few success stories to see how localization works in the real world. These companies didn't just enter new markets —they became beloved brands by embracing local flavors, habits, and needs.

1. McDonald's: Customizing the Menu, Not the Brand

McDonald's has made a global empire out of burgers and fries, but what makes it unique is how they've customized their menu for each region without compromising their brand. From the McPaneer in India to the Ebi (shrimp) Burger in Japan, McDonald's understands that taste preferences vary widely across cultures. By creating menu items that align with local tastes, they've managed to build a brand that feels both global and local.

- **Example**: In India, where a large segment of the population doesn't eat beef, McDonald's introduced a fully vegetarian menu option and tweaked their kitchen setups to keep vegetarian and non-vegetarian items separate. This commitment to local dietary preferences earned McDonald's a loyal following in India.

Lesson Learned: McDonald's success shows that you don't need to change your brand to fit in. Customize what you offer while staying true to who you are.

2. IKEA: Adapting for Assembly

When IKEA entered the Indian market, they realized that their signature flat-pack, self-assembly model wasn't going to resonate as strongly as it had in other regions. Indian consumers often prefer pre-assembled furniture, and many aren't used to the DIY approach. So IKEA took note and introduced an assembly service, ensuring that customers could enjoy IKEA's affordable furniture without the hassle of putting it together.

- **Example**: IKEA even adjusted the layout of its stores in India to reflect local shopping patterns, making the experience more intuitive for Indian customers. By adapting both the product and the shopping experience, IKEA made itself a more natural fit for the market.

Lesson Learned: Sometimes a tweak to your core product is necessary. The more you align with local preferences, the more appealing your product becomes.

3. Starbucks: Blending Global Brand with Local Tastes

Starbucks may be known for its American coffeehouse vibe, but when they went global, they quickly learned to incorporate local flavors into their menu. In Japan, they introduced matcha-flavored beverages, and in China, they added a Red Bean Green Tea Frappuccino. These localized drinks aren't just novelties—they're crafted with flavors that have cultural significance, making Starbucks feel like a local experience with an international flair.

- **Example**: Starbucks in China even adjusted its store layouts to create a more relaxed, communal atmosphere, recognizing that many customers come to the coffee shop as a social outing rather than a quick caffeine fix. The result? Starbucks has become a social destination for Chinese consumers.

Lesson Learned: You don't have to compromise your brand identity to fit in. Adding local flavors and making subtle adjustments to the experience can make your product feel uniquely relevant.

Tips for Effective Localization

Ready to get started with your own localization journey? Here are some tips to help make your product feel at home in any market.

1. Hire Local Experts

Nobody knows the local market better than someone who lives in it. Local experts can provide invaluable insights into customer preferences, language nuances, and cultural expectations. They can help you avoid missteps and ensure your localization efforts hit the mark.

2. Run Focus Groups

Focus groups are a great way to test your product with real people from the region you're targeting. Gather feedback, ask about preferences, and don't shy away from making adjustments based on what you learn. Consumers appreciate a brand that listens.

3. Test Your Marketing Campaigns

Test your marketing materials to make sure your message resonates. A campaign that works in one country might not work elsewhere, so tweak your messaging, visuals, and tone until they feel just right for each market.

4. Stay Flexible and Ready to Adapt

Localization isn't a one-and-done deal. As markets evolve, so should your approach. Stay flexible, keep listening to your customers, and be prepared to adapt to changing trends or new preferences. The best localized brands are always learning and adjusting.

Final Thoughts: The Art of Making Your Brand Feel Like Home

Localization is about making your brand feel like it belongs, no matter where you go. It's not about reinventing yourself at every turn, but rather about adapting the things that matter—like language, lifestyle fit, and buying habits—to make your product or service feel familiar and relevant.

When you take the time to localize, you're doing more than just selling a product. You're building relationships, showing respect, and ultimately becoming a part of the community. And that's how you turn a global business into a brand people love on a local level.

So, as you step into new markets, keep your focus on making your brand feel like home. With the right adjustments, a little flexibility, and a deep respect for local customs, you're well on your way to creating something that people everywhere will embrace.

CHAPTER 6: IDENTIFYING THE INFRASTRUCTURE

Needed for a Gold Rush

So, you've found a market with all the right signs of a global Gold Rush. But before you set up shop, there's a crucial question to answer: Does the infrastructure support your vision? Infrastructure might not be the most glamorous part of international expansion, but it's the backbone that determines whether your business can actually function—and thrive—on the ground.

Infrastructure goes beyond just roads and bridges; it's the logistics networks, technology access, and foundational elements that make or break your ability to reach customers and deliver value. In developing regions, where infrastructure can be a mixed bag, understanding what's in place (and what isn't) becomes essential. In this chapter, we'll explore why infrastructure matters, how to assess what you need, and some practical strategies for building partnerships to fill in the gaps.

Logistics: The Arteries of Your Operation

Let's start with logistics—the system that gets your products from point A to point B. In developed markets, logistics can be as straightforward as choosing a shipping provider. But in emerging markets, this process can be far more complex. Traffic, poor road quality, or even seasonal weather patterns can affect delivery times, not to mention regional differences in customs and distribution channels.

Having a good grasp on the local logistics scene means you can get products to your customers on time and maintain a reliable reputation. Look at existing delivery networks, available warehousing options, and local transportation methods. And remember, last-mile delivery (the final leg of the journey to customers) is often the trickiest part. In areas where infrastructure is limited, innovative solutions—like using local couriers or even bicycles—can be your best bet.

- **Example**: Amazon in India recognized that traditional logistics wouldn't work in rural areas, so they partnered with local delivery networks and even hired local couriers to ensure packages reached remote customers. By leveraging local networks, Amazon was able to extend its reach well beyond major cities.

Lesson Learned: Logistics is more than just trucks and warehouses. Understanding the nuances of local delivery and distribution channels will help you build a reliable supply chain that reaches all corners of your new market.

Technology Access: The Foundation for Digital Success

In today's digital age, technology access is everything. But here's the catch—while you might be used to seamless, high-speed internet and widespread smartphone usage, that's not always the case in developing regions. Connectivity varies widely, and if your business relies on digital transactions, mobile apps, or online customer service, you'll need to ensure your market has the tech foundation to support it.

Start by assessing the internet penetration rate, smartphone ownership, and digital literacy in the region. If connectivity is limited, think about ways to simplify your technology or offer offline options. For instance, SMS-based services are widely accessible and popular in areas where internet access may be patchy. Additionally, consider working with local telecom providers or exploring partnerships with mobile payment systems if digital payments are essential to your business.

- **Example**: In Africa, M-Pesa built a mobile money service that works on basic cell phones without requiring internet access. This innovation allowed millions to access financial services through SMS, proving that you can offer tech-driven services even in low-connectivity regions with the right adjustments.

Lesson Learned: Don't assume everyone has the same tech access you're used to. Assess connectivity and device access in the region, and adapt your product to make it accessible for everyone.

Local Infrastructure: From Roads to Warehousing

Local infrastructure doesn't just cover logistics and tech; it also includes warehousing, power reliability, and transportation. In markets with underdeveloped infrastructure, you may need to get creative with your approach. Warehousing near key cities, securing reliable suppliers, and finding efficient transportation options are all critical steps to ensuring your business runs smoothly.

When assessing infrastructure, look at the basics:

1. **Road Quality and Accessibility**: If poor roads delay shipments, consider setting up mini-distribution centers in key locations to reduce travel times.
2. **Power Reliability**: In regions with frequent power outages, you may need backup power sources to keep operations running smoothly.
3. **Local Distribution Channels**: Instead of relying on international networks, find local distributors who know the territory and can navigate it with ease.
- **Example**: Coca-Cola's success in Africa is a prime ex-

ample of infrastructure ingenuity. They've established local bottling plants across the continent and work with a vast network of local distributors to ensure their products reach even the most remote areas. By adapting to the infrastructure limitations of each region, Coca-Cola has built one of the most efficient supply chains in Africa.

Lesson Learned: Infrastructure varies greatly, and what works in one place may not work in another. Build flexibility into your setup and consider partnering with local providers to enhance reliability.

Strategies for Assessing Infrastructure Needs

Identifying what infrastructure you need to support your business involves a blend of research, testing, and partnership. Here are some practical strategies to help you assess the lay of the land and determine your needs.

1. Do a Thorough Market Assessment

A market assessment helps you see the current state of infrastructure and gauge how well it can support your operations. Look at key infrastructure indicators—such as internet access, transportation, power reliability, and availability of warehousing. Gather insights through industry reports, local contacts, and market research agencies that specialize in the region.

2. Test the Waters with a Pilot Program

If you're unsure about infrastructure limitations, consider running a pilot program before fully committing. By launching a smaller-scale version of your business, you can test your logistics, technology, and distribution methods in real-time. This allows you to identify any bottlenecks and adjust before scaling up.

- **Example**: When Alibaba first expanded outside China, they tested logistics in a few select regions before scaling. This trial period allowed them to identify issues in international shipping, adapt their distribution methods, and fine-tune their approach for broader expansion.

3. Partner with Local Companies

Local partners are invaluable when it comes to navigating infrastructure challenges. They have a deeper understanding of the region's logistics, tech access, and distribution networks. Consider partnerships with local suppliers, logistics firms, or even telecom companies to leverage their resources and expertise.

4. Plan for Contingencies

In developing markets, things don't always go as planned. Delays, power outages, and last-minute roadblocks can be part of the landscape. Having contingency plans—like backup power sources, alternative suppliers, and multiple delivery options—will help keep your operations resilient.

Collaborating with Local Partners to Bridge Gaps

If you find infrastructure lacking in key areas, don't throw in the towel—find local allies. Partnering with companies that already have a presence in the market can help bridge these gaps and ensure smooth operations. Local businesses understand the nuances of the region, from traffic patterns to peak shopping times, and their experience can be invaluable.

Types of Local Partners to Consider

1. **Logistics Providers**: Local logistics companies know how to navigate roads, warehouses, and last-mile delivery. They can handle complexities specific to the region, saving you time and resources.
2. **Telecom Companies**: If your product relies on digital connectivity, telecom partnerships can help ensure

your customers have reliable access. Many telecom providers in developing markets offer mobile payment solutions, making them ideal partners for businesses entering digital-based industries.

3. **Suppliers and Distributors**: Local suppliers have established networks and are familiar with regional demand patterns. Working with them gives you a direct link to the market, helping to streamline your supply chain and make your brand a local favorite.

- **Example**: When Walmart entered Mexico, they partnered with local suppliers to align their products with the Mexican market. By collaborating with trusted local suppliers, Walmart was able to offer products that felt familiar and met the preferences of Mexican consumers, making the transition smoother and earning local trust.

Lesson Learned: Local partners can be your secret weapon for overcoming infrastructure challenges. They bring experience, expertise, and a network that can make your entry into the market far easier.

Final Thoughts: Building a Strong Foundation for Global Success

Infrastructure is the backbone of any successful venture, and understanding what's in place (and what isn't) is essential for international growth. Logistics, technology access, and local distribution networks are more than just practical considerations—they're the elements that will support your vision in a brand-new market. By assessing infrastructure needs, testing strategies, and collaborating with local partners, you're setting up your business for a smoother expansion.

Think of infrastructure as your foundation. Get it right, and you're ready to build something that lasts, no matter the region. Get it wrong, and you'll find yourself running in circles, held back by obstacles you might have avoided with a little research and the right connections. So take the time to understand the infrastructure landscape, plan carefully, and connect with local experts. When you do, your Gold Rush is just getting started.

Part III: Entering the Market with a Strategic Edge

CHAPTER 7: BUILDING AN ENTRY STRATEGY

Alright, you've scouted a promising market, checked the infrastructure, and now you're ready to dive in. But before you cannonball into unknown waters, let's talk about strategy. Specifically, your entry strategy. Different markets call for different approaches, and choosing the right one can make the difference between smooth sailing and getting caught in rough waters.

In this chapter, we'll break down the main market entry strategies—from direct investment to partnerships and franchising—so you can pick the one that fits your goals and the region you're targeting. We'll also explore best practices for testing the waters with pilot programs, giving you a way to assess and fine-tune your approach before fully committing. Think of it as the map that'll guide you toward success without missing any turns.

Strategy 1: Direct Investment—All In, All Control

Direct investment is the "all in" approach. When you go the direct investment route, you're essentially setting up shop from scratch—building your own facilities, hiring your own team, and taking complete control over operations. This approach requires a larger upfront investment and a higher level of commitment, but it also gives you the most control over your brand, products, and customer experience.

Direct investment is ideal if you're entering a market with strong potential for long-term growth, and you want to establish a significant presence. However, keep in mind that this option comes with added risks. You're managing everything yourself, so if something goes sideways, you're the one holding the bag.

- **Example**: Apple's expansion into China is a classic case of direct investment. Instead of partnering with local retailers, Apple built its own stores, hired local staff, and maintained control over every aspect of its brand. This approach allowed Apple to create a consistent experience worldwide, but it also required a substantial investment and careful navigation of Chinese regulations.

When to Use It: Direct investment works well when you're confident about the market's potential and want full control over your brand. It's also a good choice if you have the resources to make a substantial initial investment and plan to stick around for the long haul.

Strategy 2: Partnerships—Teaming Up for Success

If direct investment feels too risky or resource-heavy, a partnership could be your best bet. Partnering with a local company allows you to leverage their knowledge, networks, and resources, making it easier to navigate regulatory hurdles, connect with local customers, and establish trust. Partnerships can take various forms, from joint ventures to strategic alliances, and the structure will depend on your goals and the level of collaboration you want.

The beauty of partnerships is that they let you dip your toes into a market without going all in. By teaming up with a local player, you can test the waters, share costs, and reduce risks. Just make sure you choose a partner who shares your vision and has a solid reputation—your success depends on their reliability.

- **Example**: Starbucks used partnerships to expand in India by teaming up with Tata Global Beverages. Tata brought local expertise, distribution networks, and consumer insights, while Starbucks brought the brand and coffee culture. Together, they established a strong foothold in a competitive market.

When to Use It: Partnerships are ideal when you want local support, don't want to bear the full risk, or when regulations make it challenging for foreign companies to operate independently. They're especially helpful in markets with cultural or regulatory complexities where local knowledge is invaluable.

Strategy 3: Franchising—Empowering Local Entrepreneurs

Franchising is like the "rented empire" approach. Instead of managing everything yourself, you empower local entrepreneurs to run their own outlets under your brand. In this model, you provide the brand, operational guidelines, and support, while the franchisees handle the day-to-day management, covering most of the costs themselves. It's a lower-risk way to enter new markets, as franchisees bear much of the financial burden and have a vested interest in making the business work.

Franchising is ideal for brands with a well-established, replicable model (think fast food or retail chains). The downside? You sacrifice some control, which means you'll need to set clear brand standards and monitor franchisees to ensure they're delivering the experience you want.

- **Example**: McDonald's is a textbook example of successful franchising. With a standardized menu and operational system, McDonald's has franchise locations across the globe. This approach lets them expand rapidly with minimal risk and capital investment, while local franchisees manage operations.

When to Use It: Franchising works best when you have a proven, scalable business model that can be replicated easily. It's an excellent choice for consumer-facing brands, especially in food, retail, or services, where consistency and brand recognition are key.

Strategy 4: Licensing—Selling the Right to Your Brand

Licensing is a lower-commitment option where you grant another company the right to manufacture or sell your products under your brand name. Think of it as renting out your brand without the full involvement of franchising or partnership. Licensing lets you tap into new markets with minimal risk, as your licensee handles manufacturing, distribution, and sales. However, since you're not directly involved, you have limited control over quality and customer experience.

This approach works well for companies looking to expand quickly or test demand in a market with minimal resources. Just be sure to set clear guidelines and choose licensees with a strong reputation to protect your brand's integrity.

- **Example**: Disney has a highly successful licensing model, allowing companies worldwide to use its characters and logos on everything from merchandise to theme parks. This strategy gives Disney a massive global presence without direct management.

When to Use It: Licensing is a great option if you want to enter a market with low commitment, quick expansion, and minimal cost. It's especially effective for intellectual property, such as products, trademarks, or tech patents, where control over brand usage can be managed through licensing agreements.

Testing the Waters: Pilot Programs and Market Testing

Before you go all-in on an entry strategy, running a pilot program or conducting market testing can give you valuable insights. Think of it as a trial run—an opportunity to test your approach, gather feedback, and make adjustments before scaling up. Here's how to make the most of your market testing phase:

1. Start Small and Scale Gradually

Choose one or two regions to start with, ideally areas with a strong potential for demand but where you can manage risks. Launch your product on a small scale, track customer feedback, monitor sales, and refine your approach based on what you learn.

- **Example**: When Uber entered China, they began with a pilot program in select cities to understand consumer behavior and local regulatory requirements. They used insights from this trial period to tailor their service and pricing models to better fit the Chinese market.

2. Gather Feedback from Real Customers

A pilot program isn't just about testing logistics; it's about hearing directly from your target audience. Use surveys, focus groups, and customer interviews to understand their preferences, pain points, and how they perceive your product. Adjust your offering based on this feedback to ensure a better fit.

3. Refine Your Marketing Approach

Market testing allows you to fine-tune your branding and messaging. Test different marketing tactics—social media campaigns, local influencers, or partnerships—to see what resonates. This phase is your chance to experiment and refine your marketing playbook before going big.

4. Monitor Key Metrics

Keep a close eye on metrics like sales, customer satisfaction, and operational costs. These will give you a clear picture of what's working and what isn't, helping you decide whether to scale up, tweak, or reconsider your entry strategy.

Lesson Learned: Market testing and pilot programs are invaluable tools for mitigating risk and making informed decisions. A trial run lets you identify and resolve potential issues early, setting you up for a smoother and more successful entry.

Final Thoughts: Choosing the Right Path for Your Market

There's no one-size-fits-all strategy for market entry, and the right approach depends on your goals, resources, and the specific market conditions. Whether you go with direct investment, partnerships, franchising, or licensing, it's essential to understand the trade-offs and select the strategy that best aligns with your brand and the region's unique dynamics.

Remember, successful entry is all about balancing control, risk, and local relevance. Choose a strategy that allows you to establish a foothold without overcommitting, and use market testing to refine your approach along the way. The right entry strategy isn't just about getting your foot in the door—it's about building a foundation for long-term success in a brand-new market.

With the right plan in place, you're well on your way to turning that next global Gold Rush into a reality. So take a deep breath, choose your path, and get ready to make your mark.

CHAPTER 8: LEVERAGING LOCAL PARTNERSHIPS AND NETWORKS

Entering a new market can be like trying to find your way in a foreign city without a map. Sure, you can figure it out on your own, but why not team up with someone who already knows the landscape? Partnering with established local businesses is one of the smartest ways to accelerate growth, build trust, and sidestep common pitfalls. After all, who better to help you break into a market than those who are already thriving in it?

In this chapter, we'll look at the value of local partnerships and networks, from speeding up market entry to navigating complex regulatory environments. We'll also cover practical tips for finding, vetting, and negotiating with potential partners or distributors so that your collaboration is built to last. Ready to make friends in high places? Let's dive in.

The Benefits of Local Partnerships: More Than Just a Shortcut

Teaming up with local businesses isn't just a shortcut—it's a strategy. Think of a partnership as your express pass to insights, infrastructure, and networks that would otherwise take years to build. Here are some of the biggest advantages of working with local partners:

1. **Cultural and Market Knowledge**: Local partners know the region's cultural nuances, consumer preferences, and business etiquette. They can help you avoid common missteps and offer valuable insights into how to tailor your offering to local tastes.
2. **Established Customer Base**: An established partner already has a customer base that knows and trusts them. This means you can piggyback on their reputation and reach new customers faster than if you were to start from scratch.
3. **Navigating Regulations and Bureaucracy**: Local partners are often familiar with the regulatory landscape, and they can help you manage permits, licenses, and other red tape. This is especially valuable in regions with complex or opaque regulatory systems.
4. **Cost Sharing and Resource Access**: Partnerships allow you to share costs, access their logistics networks, and leverage shared resources. This can save you a significant amount of money and make scaling up faster and more affordable.
- **Example**: When Walmart entered Mexico, they partnered with Cifra, a leading Mexican retailer, instead of going solo. Cifra's established presence, local knowledge, and existing infrastructure helped Walmart become one of Mexico's largest retailers. By leveraging Cifra's resources, Walmart expanded more efficiently and built credibility in the Mexican market.

Lesson Learned: A strong local partner can be your most valuable asset in a new market, providing not just access, but a deep well of insights and resources to drive growth.

Finding the Right Partner: Knowing What to Look For

Not all partnerships are created equal, and finding the right partner requires a clear understanding of what you're looking for. Here are some key factors to consider when scouting potential partners:

1. **Reputation and Credibility**: Your partner's reputation reflects on you. Look for a partner with a solid reputation, ethical business practices, and a proven track record in the region. A trustworthy partner not only opens doors but also enhances your brand's credibility.
2. **Industry Alignment**: Look for a partner who understands your industry and shares your vision. If your partner's goals and values align with yours, it's easier to create a harmonious collaboration. For example, if you're in tech, partnering with an established local tech distributor or platform makes sense.
3. **Complementary Strengths**: The best partnerships are those where both parties bring something valuable to the table. If your partner has local market expertise, distribution channels, or government connections, they can help bridge any gaps you may have in your market entry strategy.
4. **Customer Base and Network**: Ideally, your partner should already have access to your target audience. They should have a network that can help expand your reach and build trust with customers who may not yet be familiar with your brand.
- **Example**: Starbucks entered India by partnering with Tata Global Beverages, a company with a strong local presence and deep knowledge of the Indian beverage market. Tata's distribution network and established reputation helped Starbucks enter India with credibility, providing Starbucks with access to an audience that trusted the Tata name.

Lesson Learned: Don't just choose a partner based on convenience. Look for alignment in values, industry knowledge, and strengths to create a balanced partnership that benefits both sides.

Vetting Potential Partners: Look Before You Leap

Choosing a partner isn't just about a good first impression. Vetting potential partners thoroughly can help prevent misunderstandings and conflicts down the line. Here's how to evaluate a potential partner effectively:

1. **Background Check**: Conduct a thorough background check to confirm their business practices, financial stability, and legal standing. Look for any history of legal issues, poor business practices, or financial instability.
2. **Evaluate Their Track Record**: How long has the partner been in business? What kind of reputation do they have with customers and competitors? A long-standing and reputable partner is likely to be more reliable than a newcomer.
3. **Ask for References**: Talk to previous partners or clients to get a sense of what it's like to work with them. References can provide insights into the partner's reliability, ethics, and ability to meet commitments.
4. **Look at Financial Health**: Financial stability is crucial, especially in a partnership. Review their financial statements, assess their ability to handle growth, and ensure they're capable of meeting the obligations of the partnership.
- **Example**: Before Netflix partnered with Indian telecom companies to offer mobile-friendly streaming plans, they conducted extensive due diligence on potential partners. By evaluating the financial stability, user base, and reputation of telecom providers, Netflix ensured they were teaming up with partners who could deliver a smooth experience to local consumers.

Lesson Learned: Take your time vetting partners. A thorough vetting process reduces risks and ensures you're partnering with someone who can stand the test of time.

Negotiating with Partners: Setting the Foundation for Success

A successful partnership requires clear terms, mutual respect, and an understanding of each other's goals. Here are some best practices for negotiating partnerships that create win-win outcomes:

1. **Define Clear Objectives and Expectations**: From the start, establish what each side expects from the partnership. Outline your goals, responsibilities, and the value each partner brings. This clarity helps avoid misunderstandings and keeps both sides aligned.
2. **Set Performance Benchmarks**: Identify key performance indicators (KPIs) that will measure the partnership's success. Benchmarks help keep both sides accountable and allow for adjustments as needed.
3. **Determine the Scope of the Partnership**: Define the limits of the partnership, including the specific products, services, and regions involved. This keeps the partnership focused and prevents scope creep, where one party expects more than was originally agreed upon.
4. **Negotiate Exit Clauses and Conflict Resolution**: Plan for potential disagreements by setting up exit clauses, conflict resolution processes, and terms for ending the partnership. These safeguards ensure that if things don't go as planned, both parties can part ways without legal issues or hard feelings.
5. **Agree on Financial Terms**: Ensure financial transparency and outline payment terms, profit-sharing arrangements, and any investment obligations upfront. This clarity will prevent conflicts over money and ensure both parties feel fairly compensated.
- **Example**: When Walmart expanded into China, they partnered with JD.com, an e-commerce giant with strong local knowledge. By clearly defining their

shared goals, performance metrics, and responsibilities, Walmart and JD.com created a mutually beneficial partnership that supported Walmart's entry into the competitive Chinese e-commerce space.

Lesson Learned: Negotiation isn't just about getting the best deal; it's about building a foundation of trust, transparency, and mutual respect. The more effort you put into negotiating clear terms, the smoother your partnership will run.

Final Thoughts: The Power of Local Partnerships and Networks

In a new market, partnerships and networks aren't just helpful—they're essential. A strong local partner gives you access to networks, insights, and resources that would otherwise be hard to come by, and they help you avoid the classic pitfalls that trip up many international ventures.

But remember, a good partnership is a two-way street. By choosing the right partner, vetting them carefully, and negotiating clear terms, you're setting up a relationship that can accelerate growth, build trust with local customers, and pave the way for long-term success.

So as you step into a new market, think of partnerships as your most valuable asset. With the right people by your side, you're not just another foreign company—you're part of the community, working with people who know the region and are as invested in your success as you are.

CHAPTER 9: FUNDING YOUR INTERNATIONAL EXPANSION

You've got your strategy, your infrastructure plan, and maybe even a few local partnerships lined up. But there's one thing left to tackle: funding. Expanding internationally is exciting, but let's be honest—it's not cheap. Setting up shop in a new market requires capital, and the good news is that there are multiple ways to fund your global ambitions.

In this chapter, we'll explore various funding options to help turn your expansion dreams into reality. From foreign direct investment and venture capital to local banks and development organizations, we'll dive into each source, breaking down how to access these funds and when each option makes the most sense. Let's get into it.

1. Foreign Direct Investment (FDI): Playing the Long Game

Foreign Direct Investment (FDI) is when a company or individual from one country makes a substantial investment in a business located in another country. Think of it as the "big league" funding option, where foreign investors put capital into your business with the expectation of long-term growth. FDI is often used for larger projects, like building facilities or acquiring existing businesses.

For businesses with big ambitions, FDI can provide significant funding and help you gain a strong foothold in the new market. However, the process of attracting foreign investment requires a clear business plan, market research, and potentially government approval, depending on the country.

- **Example**: India has seen a surge in FDI in recent years, especially in the tech and e-commerce sectors. Amazon and Walmart have both invested heavily in India's market, recognizing its growth potential and aligning with India's FDI policies to create jobs and infrastructure.

When to Use It: FDI is best suited for businesses with substantial growth potential or for those planning to build a physical presence (like factories or stores) in the target market. It's an ideal choice for long-term investors looking to establish a major footprint.

2. Venture Capital (VC): High Growth, High Ambitions

Venture capital (VC) funding is a popular option for startups and high-growth companies, especially those in tech or innovative industries. Venture capitalists invest in businesses with the potential for rapid growth and are usually willing to take on more risk than traditional banks or investors. The catch? They typically expect substantial returns, which can mean giving up equity and some control over business decisions.

The VC route works well for companies entering dynamic or fast-growing markets, especially if they're introducing new technology or unique products. Keep in mind, though, that VCs look for businesses with scalable models, clear growth plans, and the ability to compete in high-stakes markets.

- **Example**: Southeast Asia's e-commerce and tech startup scene has boomed in recent years, with companies like Grab and Gojek securing large amounts of

VC funding to fuel their rapid expansion across multiple countries in the region.

When to Use It: VC funding is a solid choice if you have a high-growth, scalable business and are prepared to give up some equity for fast-tracked growth. It's especially useful for tech and innovation-driven businesses with global potential.

3. Government Grants: Leveraging Public Support

Many governments offer grants and incentives to encourage foreign businesses to invest locally, create jobs, or introduce new technology. These grants often come in the form of tax breaks, subsidies, or even direct cash injections, and they're typically designed to support specific industries like renewable energy, tech, manufacturing, or healthcare.

The upside? Government grants are essentially "free money," and you don't have to repay them. The downside? They're often highly competitive, with rigorous application processes and specific criteria. You'll need a strong proposal to show how your business aligns with the government's objectives.

- **Example**: In the EU, programs like Horizon Europe provide funding for businesses focused on research, sustainability, and innovation. These grants have helped companies expand across borders, fostering growth in sectors that align with the EU's goals, like green energy and digital technology.

When to Use It: Government grants are ideal if you're in an industry that aligns with national interests (like green energy or innovation) and have the patience to navigate a detailed application process. It's also a good choice if your project has a clear social or environmental benefit.

4. Local Banks and Micro-Lenders: Financing with a Local Edge

Local banks and micro-lenders can be fantastic funding sources, especially if you're targeting smaller projects or looking to grow incrementally. Unlike larger investors, local banks often have a vested interest in supporting businesses that stimulate their own economy. Additionally, they may offer loans tailored to local businesses, including flexible terms or lower interest rates.

Micro-lenders, in particular, focus on providing small loans to businesses in developing regions. They're often more accessible than banks, with a streamlined application process and a focus on community-based businesses. However, micro-loans tend to be smaller than traditional loans, so they're more suitable for funding operational expenses rather than major expansions.

- **Example**: In Latin America, many entrepreneurs turn to micro-lenders for funding. Organizations like Kiva and Grameen Bank offer micro-loans that help small businesses grow without the need for large-scale investment.

When to Use It: Local banks and micro-lenders are great for small to medium-sized projects or for businesses entering developing regions where capital requirements may be lower. They're ideal if you're looking for a community-driven funding option with a local focus.

5. International Development Organizations: Funding with a Purpose

Organizations like the International Finance Corporation (IFC), the World Bank, and regional development banks are major sources of funding for businesses entering developing or underserved markets. These organizations are often interested in projects that create jobs, boost economic growth, or tackle social challenges, and they offer financing options ranging from loans and grants to equity investments.

One big advantage of development organizations is that they're mission-driven, which means they're open to funding businesses that might not fit traditional funding molds, as long as there's a clear social or economic benefit. However, they often have strict criteria for funding and a rigorous evaluation process.

- **Example**: The African Development Bank has funded numerous initiatives in Africa, from renewable energy projects to infrastructure development, providing capital for companies that support regional growth and economic stability.

When to Use It: Development organizations are ideal if your business aims to make a positive social or economic impact. This funding option is particularly well-suited to projects that support regional growth, create jobs, or improve infrastructure.

Leveraging Your Funding Options: Building a Smart Strategy

Now that we've covered your main funding options, let's talk about how to leverage them strategically. Here's how to make the most of these funding sources and ensure your international expansion is on solid financial ground.

1. Mix and Match Funding Sources

Don't feel like you need to rely on just one source of funding. Many companies find success by combining multiple funding streams, such as pairing a government grant with local bank financing or securing VC funding while applying for development loans. This approach gives you more flexibility and helps diversify your financial backing.

2. Start with Pilot-Scale Funding

If you're testing the waters in a new market, consider starting with smaller-scale funding options. Micro-lenders or local banks are excellent choices for pilot programs. Once you've validated demand and gathered initial data, you can leverage this success to attract larger funding from VCs or development organizations.

3. Use Local Funding to Build Local Credibility

In many regions, securing local funding is more than just a financial boost—it's a trust builder. Working with local banks, investors, or even government grants demonstrates that your business is committed to the region and trusted by local institutions. This can enhance your brand's credibility and make it easier to connect with consumers and partners.

4. Align Funding with Your Expansion Goals

Different funding sources have different strengths. Align your choice of funding with your specific goals for the region. For example, if you're aiming for fast growth, VC funding may be your best bet. If you're focusing on a sustainable, long-term presence, FDI or development organization funding may be more appropriate.

Lesson Learned: Strategic funding isn't just about finding the cash—it's about picking the right partners, balancing your options, and aligning your funding with your goals for sustainable growth.

Final Thoughts: Fueling Your Global Ambitions

Funding is the fuel that powers your journey from local to global, and with the right financial strategy, there's no limit to how far you can go. Whether you're securing foreign direct investment, tapping into government grants, or working with local banks, each funding source brings unique advantages and challenges.

Ultimately, your success in securing funding depends on understanding your business needs, aligning with the right funding partners, and staying adaptable as your market entry plan evolves. Expansion may come with a hefty price tag, but with a smart funding strategy, you'll be well on your way to turning that global vision into a profitable reality.

Part IV: Establishing and Growing Your Global Presence

CHAPTER 10: SCALING SUCCESSFULLY ACROSS BORDERS

Alright, you've landed your first international clients, maybe even set up a local office, and things are heating up. Now comes the real challenge: keeping your business smooth, steady, and successful as it expands into new territories. Growth is exhilarating—sure, who doesn't want to be a globe-trotting business mogul? But expansion can also be a bit like spinning plates: the more you add, the harder it is to keep them all from crashing down.

In this chapter, we'll look at what it takes to grow your business without losing your mind (or your quality standards). We'll dig into sustainable scaling, supply chain secrets, and how to keep your customers happy in a whole new time zone. Because, honestly, scaling across borders isn't just about going big—it's about staying consistent, adaptable, and ready to roll with whatever quirks each market throws your way.

Growth That Won't Give You Growing Pains

Let's face it, no one sets out thinking, "I want my business to grow so fast that it breaks." But all too often, rapid expansion becomes a game of whack-a-mole, with problems popping up faster than you can fix them. Here's how to grow without the side effects of sudden success:

1. Create Processes You Can Actually Repeat

If you're winging it, you're asking for trouble. When you expand, processes need to be as close to plug-and-play as possible. Think of your business like a Starbucks—you want people to experience the same quality whether they're ordering a latte in LA or sipping tea in Tokyo. Standardize your operations, from employee training to quality checks, so you can keep things consistent wherever you go.

- **Example**: Starbucks cracked the code on this by creating training programs that ensure every barista, no matter where they are, knows how to whip up a flat white exactly the same way. They don't have to reinvent the wheel for each store, which keeps things moving smoothly.

2. Hire People Who Know the Local Scene

One of the biggest mistakes you can make is importing your management style wholesale and assuming it'll work everywhere. The locals will see right through it. Hiring local talent isn't just a nicety—it's essential. They know the ins and outs of consumer habits, cultural quirks, and the kind of customer service people expect. Plus, they'll help you avoid those "lost in translation" moments that can cost you big time.

- **Example**: Unilever doesn't mess around with its local teams. They hire local managers in every country, people who get the culture and the customers. By bringing local expertise on board, Unilever can build trust with customers and navigate new markets like a local.

3. Decide What to Centralize and What to Delegate

Global growth requires some fine-tuning between your headquarters and your new regional teams. Centralize the big stuff—like your core product or service and overall branding—but let local teams make the calls on marketing and customer service. They'll know if a quirky ad will fly or flop, and they're better positioned to decide how to handle those little tweaks that make a big difference.

- **Example**: McDonald's keeps its iconic brand and core menu items (Big Macs everywhere!) but lets franchisees adapt certain menu items to local tastes, whether that's the McPaneer in India or teriyaki burgers in Japan. It's global consistency with a local twist.

Lesson Learned: If you want sustainable growth, think like a seasoned traveler—pack only the essentials and adjust to the local scene as you go.

Keeping the Quality, No Matter Where You're Growing

Quality control is no joke. Your product or service has a reputation to uphold, and one bad review can snowball faster than you can say "refund." When you're scaling across borders, quality can be one of the trickiest things to manage, but it's also the most important.

1. Make Quality Control Non-Negotiable

Standardize your quality measures across the board. No ifs, ands, or buts. Whether you're making T-shirts, software, or sandwiches, your customers want consistency. Define your quality benchmarks clearly and check that every location—whether it's a manufacturing plant or a boutique store—knows them inside out.

- **Example**: Toyota doesn't just build cars; it builds systems. With the Toyota Production System, they ensure every factory around the world delivers the same high-quality vehicles. This level of consistency is part of what's made Toyota a powerhouse worldwide.

2. Use Tech to Keep Tabs from Afar

You can't be everywhere at once, but the beauty of today's tech is that it lets you monitor, measure, and manage quality from across the globe. Inventory management software, quality control apps, and data dashboards let you keep an eye on things without hopping on a plane every week.

- **Example**: Zara's real-time inventory system helps them spot trends, notice quality issues, and restock items fast. They know what's happening in every store at any given time, which allows them to adjust production on the fly and keep customers happy.

3. Don't Skimp on Training

You can't just send people an employee handbook and expect them to deliver top-notch service. Take the time to train teams in each country. If they understand your quality standards and the reasoning behind them, they're more likely to uphold them, even when you're not watching.

- **Example**: Apple's training programs are legendary, teaching employees not just the "how" but the "why" behind their high standards. That's why, whether you're in an Apple Store in New York or Tokyo, you get the same level of customer care.

Lesson Learned: Your product should look, feel, and perform the same everywhere. Train your people, use tech to keep an eye on quality, and make consistency your mantra.

Managing Your Supply Chain and Inventory Like a Pro

When you're dealing with multiple countries, managing supply chains and inventory becomes an art form. You'll need a balance of efficiency, flexibility, and adaptability to make sure every product is available where it's needed, without unnecessary delays or stockouts.

1. Don't Put All Your Eggs in One Supplier's Basket

If your entire supply chain is reliant on a single factory, warehouse, or supplier, you're a small disruption away from a big problem. Diversify your suppliers and distribution centers to reduce your exposure to any single point of failure.

- **Example**: Nestlé has multiple production sites around the world, so if there's an issue in one location, they can pivot to another. It's a key part of how they manage risk and keep product availability consistent across regions.

2. Invest in Inventory Management Tech

Managing inventory without tech is like playing darts blindfolded—you might hit the target, but you're more likely to miss. Invest in inventory management systems that provide real-time updates, track stock levels across locations, and give you insights into regional demand.

- **Example**: Amazon uses its tech muscle to forecast demand and move products to warehouses close to customers, reducing delivery times and keeping customers happy. It's one of the reasons Amazon Prime can get items to customers' doors at lightning speed.

3. Adapt Your Logistics to Fit the Local Scene

Each region has its own logistical quirks, whether it's tight urban spaces or unreliable road networks. Tailor your logistics strategy to fit local conditions—use local couriers, bikes, boats, or whatever works best to get products to your customers on time.

- **Example**: DHL customizes its logistics for each country. In some African nations, they use bikes and motorcycles to reach customers in remote areas where traditional trucks don't make sense.

Lesson Learned: Supply chains are like houseplants—they need regular care and the right environment to thrive. Diversify your supply routes, lean on tech, and adapt your logistics to keep things flowing smoothly.

Customer Service That Speaks Their Language (Literally)

Customer service is the frontline of your brand, and when you're working across borders, it's not just about getting the job done. It's about speaking your customers' language (literally and figuratively) and being sensitive to cultural nuances. Here's how to keep customer service top-notch across time zones.

1. Speak Their Language

If you're going global, so should your customer support. Language barriers can frustrate customers faster than you can say "hello." Offer support in the primary languages of your target markets, whether that's through live chat, phone, or email.

- **Example**: Airbnb has multilingual support across 30+ languages, so wherever you are, there's someone who speaks your language. This small effort makes a big difference for customer satisfaction.

2. Use Local Channels

Your customer service channels should fit the local landscape. In some places, phone calls are still the go-to, while in others, everyone's on messaging apps. Find out how your target audience prefers to communicate, and meet them there.

- **Example**: Nike uses WeChat for customer support in China, meeting consumers where they're already spending their time. It's a simple tweak, but it makes all the difference.

3. Train for Cultural Sensitivity

Customer service isn't just about solving problems; it's about understanding the customer's expectations. Train your teams on cultural differences in communication styles, preferred response times, and etiquette, so they can serve customers in a way that feels familiar and respectful.

- **Example**: American Express takes cultural training seriously, ensuring that their support teams know the norms and expectations of each market they serve. This attention to detail is part of why they're trusted worldwide.

Lesson Learned: Customer service that feels local builds loyalty. Speak their language, be available on their channels, and understand their cultural cues.

Final Thoughts on Scaling Across Borders

Growing across borders is an adventure. You're taking your business to new places, reaching new people, and building something bigger than ever. But as you go global, keep your standards close. Consistency is king, quality is queen, and customer experience is the crown jewel. Standardize what matters, adapt where you need to, and never lose sight of what made your business great in the first place.

With a bit of savvy, some solid systems, and an eye for the nuances that make each market unique, you're ready to scale like a pro—no matter where in the world you're headed.

CHAPTER 11: STAYING AGILE IN A RAPIDLY CHANGING WORLD

Congratulations! You've taken your business global, scaled across borders, and built a solid reputation. But here's the thing: global markets are like the weather—predictably unpredictable. Just when you think you've got it all figured out, a new regulation, economic shift, or shiny tech trend blows in, shaking things up and keeping everyone on their toes. The businesses that survive these twists and turns aren't the ones rooted like oaks; they're the ones bending like bamboo. In short, agility is your best friend.

In this chapter, we'll look at how to keep your business flexible in a world where change is the only constant. We'll dive into responding to economic and regulatory shifts, staying ahead of technological advancements, and using a bit of good old-fashioned adaptability to roll with whatever global markets throw your way.

Navigating Economic Shifts Without Going Under

Economic tides can turn fast, and global expansion only magnifies the impact of these shifts. Whether it's inflation, currency fluctuations, or a full-blown recession, you're going to need a strategy to keep your head above water when the economy takes a dip. Here's how to stay afloat (and maybe even thrive) during the rollercoaster that is the global economy.

1. Diversify, Diversify, Diversify

The same way smart investors don't put all their money in one stock, savvy businesses don't rely on a single market to carry them. Diversifying your customer base, suppliers, and revenue streams is the best insurance against market downturns in any one location. If one market takes a hit, the others help you balance things out.

- **Example**: Coca-Cola operates in over 200 countries. If demand dips in one region, Coca-Cola leans on revenue from others. It's why the company weathers economic storms better than many—having options makes all the difference.

2. Build a Financial Safety Net

When the economy tanks, cash flow is king. Having a rainy-day fund or access to quick financing can keep you stable when times are tough. This could be a line of credit, strategic partnerships with banks, or simply keeping some capital tucked away for emergencies.

- **Example**: Apple hoards cash like a dragon guarding gold. This cushion lets Apple ride out economic slumps, invest in new ventures, and snap up opportunities when they come up. Sometimes, keeping cash on hand is your best move in a shaky market.

3. Adjust Prices and Costs Strategically

When inflation hits or a currency devalues, those slim profit margins can disappear faster than you can say "supply chain." Consider flexible pricing models, bulk discounts for high-demand items, and tightening operational costs. Keep an eye on consumer trends too—when wallets get tight, value and affordability win the day.

- **Example**: McDonald's knows how to adjust its pricing without hurting its brand. In times of economic stress, McDonald's rolls out value meals and discounts to keep customers coming in. By tweaking its menu offerings and prices, it stays affordable and relevant without compromising quality.

Lesson Learned: Economic ups and downs are part of the global game. Spread out your risk, save some cash, and don't be afraid to flex on pricing to keep customers on board.

Dodging Regulatory Curveballs Like a Pro

Every country has its own set of rules, and sometimes they change at the drop of a hat. New tariffs, taxes, labor laws, and product standards can pop up out of nowhere and throw a wrench in your operations. Staying agile here means being proactive, informed, and, yes, a little bit crafty.

1. Keep Local Experts on Speed Dial

The best way to stay on top of regulatory shifts? Hire locals who know the system. They'll alert you to changes before they become an issue and help you navigate complex requirements. Plus, when you're working with people who understand the nuances, you're less likely to get blindsided by a law buried in the fine print.

- **Example**: Tesla's expansion into China came with a lot of regulatory hoops. Tesla hired a local team to handle everything from factory permits to tariff compliance, ensuring it had people on the ground who knew the ropes. The result? Tesla was able to ramp up production and dodge some regulatory headaches along the way.

2. Build Flexibility into Contracts

Locking yourself into rigid contracts can spell disaster if new regulations come up. Whenever possible, build flexibility into your agreements. Include clauses for renegotiation or adjust pricing if compliance costs rise—this keeps you agile without breaking promises.

- **Example**: Apple's supply chain contracts include flexible clauses that account for shifts in tariffs or production costs. This means Apple can adapt to changes without passing on costs directly to consumers, keeping everyone happy.

3. Stay in the Loop with Trade Groups and Industry Associations

Joining industry groups isn't just for networking over coffee. These organizations often get early insights into upcoming policy changes and help you make sense of regulations before they go live. Plus, you'll have allies to lobby for favorable terms when the rules are being written.

- **Example**: The American Chamber of Commerce in China provides updates and insights for U.S. companies, keeping them aware of new regulations. By staying involved, companies can adapt before changes catch them off guard.

Lesson Learned: Navigating regulatory shifts requires local expertise, flexible agreements, and staying connected to industry groups. Keeping a finger on the pulse of policy changes will save you from scrambling to adjust.

Riding the Wave of Technological Advancements

Tech changes faster than a teenage trend cycle, and keeping up isn't just smart—it's essential. Businesses that adopt new tech early gain an edge, while those that lag behind get left in the dust. Here's how to stay on the leading edge without blowing your budget on every shiny gadget that comes out.

1. Embrace the Tech That Makes You Leaner and Faster

Not all tech is created equal. The best investments are the ones that automate tedious tasks, streamline operations, and give you a better look at what's happening across your markets. ERP systems, data analytics, and AI-driven customer support? They're no longer just nice-to-haves—they're essential tools for agility.

- **Example**: Zara's fast-fashion empire relies on data analytics to spot trends and adjust inventory in real-time. By using tech to see what's selling and what's not, Zara can pivot on a dime, keeping stores stocked with what customers want.

2. Test Before You Dive In

With new tech, think of yourself as an early adopter, not a guinea pig. Don't rush to overhaul your entire system before you know it works. Start with pilot programs in select locations, test the waters, and see if the tech lives up to the hype. If it's a winner, then you can roll it out full-scale.

- **Example**: Amazon started experimenting with drone deliveries in small test markets before expanding. They worked out the kinks, gathered feedback, and refined the technology before taking it to a larger stage. Slow and steady wins the race.

3. Train Your Team to Adapt

The best tech in the world won't do you any good if your team doesn't know how to use it. Make sure your employees have the training to embrace new tools, adapt to tech changes, and spot opportunities for improvement. A culture that's open to change makes adopting new technologies a whole lot easier.

- **Example**: Google is constantly evolving its tech, but it also invests heavily in training to keep employees up-to-speed. By prioritizing education, Google ensures its team is ready to adopt the latest tools and hit the ground running.

Lesson Learned: Tech is a game-changer, but don't rush into it blind. Embrace what helps you work smarter, test before you invest big, and make sure your team is on board with the shift.

Cultivating an Adaptable Company Culture

Agility isn't just about policies and strategies; it's about mindset. A company culture that embraces change, stays curious, and encourages flexibility will be far better equipped to handle whatever curveballs the global market throws. Here's how to build a culture that can roll with the punches.

1. Encourage Experimentation (And Be Okay with Failing Fast)

If your team feels like every new idea has to be a home run, you're going to stifle innovation. Encourage small-scale experimentation, and let people know it's okay to fail fast and pivot. It's not about perfection—it's about progress.

- **Example**: Netflix built its success on a culture of experimentation. They test everything from marketing campaigns to user interfaces, ditching what doesn't work and scaling what does. This willingness to experiment keeps Netflix nimble in a crowded field.

2. Stay Curious and Keep Learning

Agility isn't a one-time achievement—it's an ongoing process. Create a culture that values learning by offering training, promoting cross-department collaboration, and encouraging people to stay on top of industry trends. The more your team knows, the better they'll be at spotting opportunities and adapting on the fly.

- **Example**: Microsoft went through a major cultural shift, embracing a "learn-it-all" mentality instead of a "know-it-all" mindset. This shift has allowed Microsoft to innovate, reinvent itself, and stay relevant.

3. Empower Your People to Make Decisions

Nothing kills agility faster than decision bottlenecks. Trust your team, and give them the authority to make decisions within their purview. Empowered employees can act fast when needed, and their insights on the ground are often your best guide to what works and what doesn't.

- **Example**: Ritz-Carlton gives its employees the freedom to spend up to $2,000 to solve guest issues without manager approval. This empowerment lets staff resolve issues quickly, keeping guests happy and operations running smoothly.

Lesson Learned: Building an adaptable culture means valuing experimentation, fostering curiosity, and empowering employees to make decisions. With these in place, you'll be ready to adapt no matter what comes your way.

Final Thoughts on Staying Agile

Going global is a wild ride, but adaptability is what keeps you on the road when it gets rocky. A nimble business can pivot around obstacles, dodge sudden drops, and accelerate when new opportunities appear. With a diverse revenue base, flexible contracts, the latest tech, and a team that's ready to roll with change, your business won't just survive a shifting world—it'll thrive.

So, keep a finger on the pulse, stay open to change, and never underestimate the power of a well-timed pivot. Agility isn't just about staying in the game; it's about leading it. With a bit of flexibility and a lot of curiosity, you'll be ready to take on whatever the future brings.

CHAPTER 12: CREATING A LONG-TERM VISION FOR INTERNATIONAL GROWTH

By now, you've learned how to tackle international markets, scale across borders, and roll with the punches. But if you really want to play the long game, you'll need a vision that stretches beyond next quarter's profits. Long-term international growth isn't just about expanding your footprint; it's about planting roots that turn your brand into a global staple, a name people know, trust, and look for wherever they are.

In this chapter, we're talking big picture—the kind of vision that lets your brand stand tall through trends, economic storms, and market shifts. We'll explore lessons from iconic global brands that grew sustainably, stayed relevant, and mastered the art of long-term thinking. Because while it's fun to ride the waves of rapid growth, the real winners are the ones who know how to build an enduring legacy.

Building a Brand People Can Trust Worldwide

Let's start with the obvious: if you're going to stick around for the long haul, people have to trust you. And in a world where trust can take years to build and seconds to lose, every step matters. It's not enough to just be recognizable—you want to be respected. Here's how to build a reputation that lasts.

1. Commit to Consistency

Consistency is key to any strong brand, especially when you're spreading across time zones and cultures. Customers want to know that your product or service will deliver the same quality and experience, no matter where they find you. Standardize what makes your brand "you," and make sure every team member gets it, from the marketing reps in Mexico City to the floor staff in Frankfurt.

- **Example**: Coca-Cola has kept its taste, branding, and even bottle shape consistent around the world. Sure, they tweak things here and there for local markets (hello, cherry flavor in Japan), but at its core, a Coke is a Coke, and that familiarity makes them a global staple.

2. Stand for Something Bigger Than Business

Want customers to stick with you for decades? Stand for something that goes beyond what you sell. Customers love brands that care about the same things they do, whether that's environmental sustainability, social responsibility, or innovation. When people see your brand making a positive impact, it resonates on a deeper level, creating loyalty that lasts.

- **Example**: Patagonia built its brand on environmental activism and sustainable fashion. They make a great product, but they also advocate for the planet, leading by example and inspiring loyalty from customers who care about environmental issues.

3. Embrace Transparency and Accountability

No one expects a company to be perfect, but they do expect honesty. When something goes wrong, admit it, and show how you're going to make it right. A global brand that's open about its missteps (and what it's doing to fix them) will gain respect faster than one that tries to sweep things under the rug.

- **Example**: Johnson & Johnson faced a major crisis when Tylenol was tampered with in the 1980s. Instead of hiding, they pulled every bottle from shelves, revamped their safety measures, and rebuilt trust with consumers. The move paid off, and Tylenol came back stronger than ever.

Lesson Learned: Building trust isn't about flashy campaigns; it's about being there for the long run, standing for something, and doing the right thing—even when it's hard.

Planning for Growth That Outlasts Trends

Trends come and go, but a sustainable global brand sticks around. To make your business a long-term player, you'll need a growth strategy that focuses on durability over flash. Here's how to avoid the hype trap and focus on strategies that age well.

1. Don't Chase Every Trend (But Don't Ignore Them Either)

When a trend pops up, it's tempting to dive in headfirst. But long-term growth means knowing when to hold back. Jumping on every fad can dilute your brand and confuse customers. Instead, keep an eye on trends, and only go after the ones that align with your core values and purpose.

- **Example**: Nike doesn't jump on every new sneaker trend—they focus on innovation that aligns with performance and style. By sticking to what they do best, they've stayed relevant without compromising their brand.

2. Invest in Timeless Innovation

True innovation doesn't just follow the trend—it shapes it. Focus on innovations that improve your core product, enhance customer experience, or solve real problems for your market. It's not about being first; it's about being the best at what actually matters to your customers.

- **Example**: Apple's focus on seamless design, intuitive interfaces, and user-centric products made it a global icon. They weren't the first to invent the smartphone or tablet, but they redefined what those devices could be by prioritizing quality and functionality.

3. Cultivate a Culture of Learning and Adaptability

Long-lasting brands aren't afraid to evolve. Create a culture that values learning, continuous improvement, and adaptability. Encourage your team to stay curious, seek new knowledge, and always be on the lookout for ways to improve. When your entire organization is built around growth, the brand itself becomes stronger, more flexible, and ready for anything.

- **Example**: Microsoft transformed itself by embracing a "learn-it-all" rather than a "know-it-all" mindset. This cultural shift allowed the company to pivot and innovate, turning it into one of the most valuable brands in the world. Microsoft's ability to adapt has made it resilient and future-proof.

Lesson Learned: Longevity comes from knowing who you are, evolving without losing focus, and investing in meaningful innovation. Trends are fine, but building a brand that outlasts them is even better.

Learning from the Brands That Got It Right

Every long-standing global brand has something to teach us about growth, resilience, and keeping the big picture in mind. Let's take a look at a few legends and what we can learn from their success.

1. Unilever: Mastering Local Adaptation with Global Consistency

Unilever is one of the world's largest consumer goods companies, with products in nearly every corner of the globe. Their secret? They maintain brand consistency, but adapt to local tastes and values. Instead of enforcing a one-size-fits-all approach, Unilever empowers its regional teams to make decisions based on local insights. It's the reason why Dove ads in Brazil might look different than in the UK, but the core message of self-confidence remains the same.

Lesson: Long-term growth requires consistency, but don't be afraid to give each region its own personality. A local touch makes a global brand feel close to home.

2. IKEA: Affordability, Adaptability, and Purpose

IKEA started with a simple vision: affordable, stylish furniture for everyone. Decades later, they're still growing because they've stuck to that mission while innovating on the execution. From developing sustainable materials to creating furniture tailored to small apartments in urban markets, IKEA adapts without losing sight of its core purpose. It's why they've become a household name in so many countries.

Lesson: Know your purpose, and let it guide every innovation, every market, every strategy. When your purpose drives growth, it's much easier to stay relevant across regions and generations.

3. LEGO: Building Creativity Across Generations

LEGO has been around since the 1930s, and its success lies in its simplicity and universal appeal. But even LEGO had to evolve to stay relevant. They expanded into movies, video games, and theme parks, creating an entire ecosystem around their iconic bricks. By adapting to changing tastes while staying true to their creative roots, LEGO became a brand that kids (and adults) across the world cherish.

Lesson: Sometimes the key to longevity is building an ecosystem, not just a product. If you create experiences around your brand, you'll become a bigger part of people's lives—and not just for a season.

Crafting Your Own Long-Term Vision

Now that we've covered the foundations of long-term growth, it's time to think about your own brand's future. Here are a few steps to get you started on crafting a vision that lasts:

1. **Define Your Brand's Core Purpose**: Why does your business exist beyond making a profit? Your purpose should resonate across borders and stand the test of time. Write it down, share it with your team, and let it guide your decisions.
2. **Set Big-Picture Goals**: Think beyond the next quarter or even the next year. Where do you want to be in five, ten, or twenty years? Set goals that align with your purpose and keep you moving in the right direction.
3. **Map Out Key Milestones**: Long-term goals can feel overwhelming without a roadmap. Break them down into milestones—significant achievements that mark your journey. This approach keeps you motivated and gives you a way to measure progress.
4. **Stay Open to Change (But Stay True to Your Core)**: Remember, agility is just as important for long-term growth as it is for short-term survival. Be ready to adapt, pivot, or experiment, but always come back to what makes your brand unique.

Example: TOMS started with a mission to give a pair of shoes to someone in need for every pair sold. This purpose-driven model grew into a global phenomenon, but TOMS didn't stop there.

They expanded into other products, keeping the mission of giving at their core. It's what has kept TOMS relevant even as they've evolved.

Lesson Learned: A long-term vision isn't a rigid plan; it's a guidepost. Keep your purpose at the center, set big goals, and be willing to adapt when necessary.

Final Thoughts on Long-Term Global Growth

Long-term growth isn't about racing to the top; it's about sticking around long after the hype fades. By building a brand people trust, committing to a purpose that matters, and staying flexible enough to adapt, you're not just expanding your business—you're creating a legacy. Remember, the brands that become icons are the ones that combine purpose with resilience and stay true to what they believe in, no matter where in the world they go.

So, dream big, think long, and stay steady. Because with the right vision and a commitment to creating something that matters, your brand won't just be another name on the market. It'll be the one people look for, rely on, and stay loyal to—no matter what.

ANDREA OLIVER

Part V: Case Studies of Modern Global Gold Rushes

CHAPTER 13: CASE STUDY — FINTECH IN AFRICA

Fintech and Africa. It might seem like an unexpected match, but in recent years, it's become one of the most transformative pairings on the planet. In a region where traditional banking infrastructure is often sparse or downright inaccessible, mobile money platforms have stepped up to bridge the gap. From giving people a safe place to store their money to enabling businesses to transact without ever setting foot in a bank, fintech has changed the game —and created enormous opportunities along the way.

In this chapter, we'll dive into how mobile money platforms transformed financial access in Africa, spurring economic growth and creating new wealth in underserved regions. And, if you're looking to enter a market with limited infrastructure, there's plenty to learn from Africa's fintech revolution.

The Backstory: A Continent Ripe for Fintech

Imagine having to travel for hours just to deposit money, or worse, hiding cash at home because there's no bank nearby. For years, this was a reality for millions across Africa. Traditional banks had little reach outside urban centers, and even within cities, branches were few and far between. The result? Limited access to savings accounts, credit, and basic financial services.

Then came mobile money—a simple, powerful solution that used the one tool everyone already had: a mobile phone. Companies like Safaricom in Kenya introduced M-Pesa, a mobile money service that lets people deposit, withdraw, and transfer money via SMS. What started as a way to send money home quickly morphed into a full-blown financial ecosystem, empowering millions to manage their finances, pay bills, and even access microloans—all without ever visiting a bank.

Lesson Learned: Sometimes the simplest solution has the biggest impact. Mobile money succeeded because it met people where they were, using a technology they already knew and trusted.

How Mobile Money Changed the Game

Mobile money didn't just provide convenience—it unlocked new opportunities across multiple sectors. Here's how it transformed Africa's financial landscape and created new avenues for growth.

1. Enabling Small Businesses to Thrive

Imagine trying to run a business with no bank account and no way to accept card payments. That was the reality for countless small and medium-sized businesses in Africa. Mobile money allowed these entrepreneurs to accept payments, manage cash flow, and track transactions—all through a mobile phone. Suddenly, owning a small shop or running a market stall became more viable, giving entrepreneurs a chance to build wealth and grow their communities.

- **Example**: In Uganda, a study found that small vendors who used mobile money saw their daily income increase by an average of 15%. By streamlining payments and reducing cash-handling risks, mobile money helped businesses become more efficient and profitable.

2. Bringing Financial Inclusion to the Masses

Before mobile money, financial services were a luxury reserved for a small percentage of the population. Today, mobile money platforms have brought financial inclusion to millions who previously had no access to banking services. People can save for emergencies, invest in their children's education, and build small businesses without ever having to handle physical cash. In a place where trust in banks was historically low, mobile money created a system that felt accessible, convenient, and reliable.

- **Example**: M-Pesa, the poster child for mobile money, now reaches over 40 million users in Africa. For many, it's more than just a money-transfer service; it's a financial lifeline that lets them save, borrow, and invest in ways they never could before.

3. Empowering Women and Underserved Communities

In many African countries, women and rural communities had even less access to financial services than their urban male counterparts. Mobile money platforms leveled the playing field, allowing women and people in remote areas to handle their finances independently. This empowerment has led to higher incomes, better health outcomes, and increased educational opportunities in underserved regions.

- **Example**: Studies show that in countries like Kenya, mobile money usage has led to a 20% reduction in poverty rates among female-headed households. Access to mobile money enabled women to participate more fully in the economy, contributing to household income and lifting their families out of poverty.

Lesson Learned: Fintech can do more than just facilitate transactions; it can be a powerful tool for social change, especially in communities that have been historically excluded from financial services.

Working Within Limited Banking Infrastructure

So, what's the secret to succeeding in a market where traditional infrastructure is lacking? Africa's fintech pioneers can tell you—it's all about flexibility, innovation, and a deep understanding of what people actually need.

1. Use What's Already There (Even If It's Just a Mobile Phone)

When you're dealing with limited infrastructure, leveraging what's already in place is crucial. Mobile money didn't rely on bank branches, ATMs, or even smartphones—it worked with basic cell phones, using SMS to handle transactions. By using technology people already had, fintech companies could avoid building costly new infrastructure and make their services accessible from day one.

- **Example**: M-Pesa didn't need internet access or expensive apps; it worked via text message, allowing even the most rural customers to transact without a hitch. This simplicity and accessibility were key to its rapid adoption.

2. Partner with Local Players Who Understand the Landscape

Africa's fintech success didn't happen in a vacuum; it was built on partnerships with mobile network operators, local governments, and community organizations. By working with people who understood the local landscape, fintech companies gained trust, improved reach, and could scale much faster than going it alone.

- **Example**: M-Pesa's success in Kenya was in part due to Safaricom's deep roots in the local community. Safaricom used its vast network of agents, many of whom were local shop owners, to handle deposits and withdrawals, making mobile money as accessible as buying a loaf of bread.

3. Design Services Around Real Needs, Not Just Trends

It's easy to get caught up in flashy tech trends, but Africa's mobile money platforms have thrived because they solve real, tangible problems. By focusing on essential services—like paying bills, saving money, and transferring funds—these platforms quickly became indispensable. People didn't adopt mobile money because it was trendy; they adopted it because it made their lives easier.

- **Example**: Mobile money providers didn't start with fancy add-ons; they started with basic transfers, then expanded to services like bill payments, microloans, and insurance. They built trust with simple, useful services, then introduced more complex offerings as demand grew.

Lesson Learned: In markets with limited infrastructure, keep it simple, solve real problems, and partner with trusted local players. Flashy tech is great, but it's the practical stuff that wins people over.

Lessons for Future Fintech Innovators

Africa's fintech story offers plenty of lessons for any business looking to operate in regions with limited infrastructure. Here's how you can apply these insights to your own venture.

1. Embrace a "Mobile-First" Mentality

If there's one thing Africa's fintech revolution has taught us, it's that mobile-first isn't just a nice idea—it's essential. Many regions with limited banking infrastructure still have widespread mobile access, so build with that in mind. Keep interfaces simple, make navigation intuitive, and ensure your services can work on low-bandwidth connections.

2. Start Small, Scale Smart

Mobile money succeeded by starting with the basics, building trust, and gradually adding more services. Think of your market entry as an onion: start with the outer layer (core needs) and peel back as you go deeper (additional services). This approach keeps you focused on what matters and reduces the risk of overextending.

3. Lean into Local Insights

A global strategy is only as good as its local execution. Lean into local insights, get feedback from people on the ground, and don't assume one-size-fits-all will work everywhere. Build relationships with local experts, invest in understanding regional nuances, and be ready to adapt.

- **Example**: Paystack, a Nigerian fintech company acquired by Stripe, grew rapidly by focusing on the specific needs of Nigerian businesses. They solved pain points specific to local merchants, creating a tailored experience that made them indispensable.

Lesson Learned: A mobile-first, user-centered approach that builds gradually and respects local insights is a recipe for success in regions with limited infrastructure.

Final Thoughts on the Fintech Gold Rush in Africa

Fintech's impact on Africa has been nothing short of revolutionary, unlocking financial access and creating wealth where there was once economic exclusion. The lesson? The "Gold Rush" opportunities are still out there; they're just waiting in places most people overlook. The secret to success in underserved markets isn't necessarily about cutting-edge technology—it's about using what's already there, partnering with the right people, and focusing on practical solutions that genuinely make life easier.

So, if you're looking to take your business somewhere new, take a page out of Africa's fintech playbook. Innovate, but keep it simple. Be mobile, be local, and above all, be useful. Because in the end, it's not just about entering a new market; it's about changing the game in a way that lasts.

CHAPTER 14: CASE STUDY — RENEWABLE ENERGY IN DEVELOPING NATIONS

Renewable energy and developing nations—two phrases that might not seem like natural partners at first glance. But in recent years, these regions have become fertile ground for renewable energy startups. With demand for clean energy surging and government support stronger than ever, developing nations are attracting entrepreneurs and investors eager to capture this "Green Gold Rush." From solar-powered grids in rural areas to wind farms in remote regions, renewable energy is lighting up the world's emerging economies in more ways than one.

In this chapter, we'll explore how renewable energy is transforming developing regions, creating jobs, and improving quality of life while making a positive environmental impact. We'll also look at strategies for navigating regulatory landscapes and building partnerships with governments—a critical move if you want to succeed in these highly-regulated and often unpredictable markets.

The Surge of Clean Energy Demand in Developing Nations

Developing nations have traditionally relied on fossil fuels to fuel their growth, but the tides are shifting fast. With rising awareness about climate change, air quality concerns, and limited access to reliable electricity, renewable energy isn't just an environmental choice—it's an economic lifeline. And unlike traditional energy sources, which are often centralized and expensive, renewable energy systems can be decentralized and relatively low-cost, making them ideal for regions that lack robust infrastructure.

Add in the fact that governments are now actively supporting renewable projects, and you have a setup that's practically begging for innovation. From tax breaks to fast-track permits, the opportunities are there. You just need to know how to seize them.

Lesson Learned: Clean energy is no longer a "nice-to-have" in developing nations—it's a necessity. When both the government and the people are rooting for renewable energy, the market potential is vast.

How Renewable Energy Startups Are Changing the Game

The renewable energy movement is doing more than just lighting up homes and businesses. It's bringing economic empowerment, environmental sustainability, and energy independence to communities that have been off the grid—both literally and figuratively.

1. Reaching the Unreachable with Microgrids

In many rural areas, traditional power grids simply aren't feasible. Enter microgrids: small, self-sufficient energy systems that can power villages, farms, and communities without needing a massive grid. These renewable-powered microgrids have become game-changers, providing reliable electricity to people who might otherwise be left in the dark.

- **Example**: In Rwanda, a company called Bboxx deploys solar-powered microgrids to bring electricity to remote areas. With affordable, pay-as-you-go options, Bboxx has made clean energy accessible to communities that were previously underserved by utility companies.

2. Empowering Small Businesses with Solar Power

Renewable energy isn't just for homes; it's also empowering small businesses in developing nations. Solar energy is particularly popular, allowing businesses to operate longer hours and access equipment that was previously out of reach. From small retail stores to farming operations, solar power is giving entrepreneurs the tools to grow their businesses sustainably.

- **Example**: In India, SELCO Solar has been providing solar-powered solutions to small businesses for decades. From lighting to refrigeration, their solar tech enables businesses to thrive without relying on unstable electricity supplies. SELCO's model shows how renewable energy can be a vehicle for economic growth in underserved areas.

3. Generating Jobs and Training a Green Workforce

Renewable energy startups don't just deliver power—they create jobs. These projects require installation, maintenance, and local customer support, which translates into employment opportunities in regions where jobs are often scarce. By training a local workforce, these companies contribute to economic growth and help ensure that the systems they install will be sustainable in the long run.

- **Example**: Solar Sister, a social enterprise in Africa, employs and trains women to become solar sales agents in their communities. This model not only provides access to renewable energy but also empowers women economically, creating jobs and promoting gender equality in underserved regions.

Lesson Learned: Renewable energy startups are doing more than just providing electricity—they're enabling growth, empowering businesses, and creating jobs. The social impact of renewable energy in developing nations goes well beyond clean power.

Navigating Regulatory Landscapes in Developing Nations

When it comes to renewable energy, regulation is both a blessing and a curse. Governments are keen to support green initiatives, but each nation has its own set of rules, incentives, and regulatory hurdles. Knowing how to navigate these landscapes is key to success.

1. Do Your Homework (Or Hire Someone Who Has)

Regulations can be a maze of permits, environmental assessments, and local bylaws. You'll need to know the rules inside and out to avoid costly delays or shutdowns. If you're venturing into a new market, hiring a local expert or legal advisor can save you time and money.

- **Example**: When Tesla planned its Gigafactory in China, it navigated regulatory hurdles by partnering with local experts. This approach allowed Tesla to secure permits and meet environmental standards faster, demonstrating the value of understanding and respecting local rules.

2. Align with Government Goals

Many developing nations are eager to boost renewable energy as part of their development goals. Aligning your project with the government's priorities—whether that's job creation, rural electrification, or carbon reduction—can increase your chances of getting approvals, funding, and public support. Show how your project will help the country achieve its targets, and you'll be much more likely to win over key stakeholders.

- **Example**: Off Grid Electric, a solar energy company in Tanzania, works closely with the Tanzanian government, aligning its goals with national energy plans. This alignment has helped Off Grid Electric secure financing and expand its impact, showing how cooperation can accelerate growth.

3. Build Relationships, Not Just Transactions

Building connections with local officials and community leaders isn't just smart—it's essential. Relationships can make or break your project, so take the time to get to know the people who can support you. Attend local events, join industry associations, and always be open to feedback. A little goodwill goes a long way in ensuring your project is welcomed.

- **Example**: Power Africa, a U.S. government-led initiative, collaborates with African governments and private-sector partners to advance clean energy projects. By fostering relationships with local stakeholders, Power Africa has been able to support dozens of renewable projects, creating a model of partnership-driven growth.

Lesson Learned: In developing regions, knowing the regulations is only part of the puzzle. To succeed, you need to align with government goals, build strong relationships, and work collaboratively with local stakeholders.

Securing Government Partnerships for Long-Term Success

Government partnerships can provide the stability and resources needed to make renewable energy projects successful in the long run. Here's how to secure those partnerships and ensure your project has staying power.

1. Seek Out Subsidies and Incentives

Many developing nations offer subsidies, tax breaks, and grants for renewable energy projects. Do your research to find out what's available, and don't be shy about applying. These incentives can lower costs, improve profitability, and help you scale faster than you could on your own.

- **Example**: Kenya offers tax incentives for renewable energy equipment, making it easier for companies like M-KOPA Solar to provide affordable solar solutions to rural customers. This support has enabled M-KOPA to expand rapidly, bringing solar energy to thousands of households.

2. Establish Public-Private Partnerships

Public-private partnerships (PPPs) are one of the most effective ways to combine resources, reduce risk, and achieve large-scale impact. When governments and private companies work together, they can share costs, overcome infrastructure challenges, and improve access to clean energy.

- **Example**: Nigeria's Energizing Education Programme (EEP) is a PPP that brings solar power to universities across Nigeria. By partnering with private energy companies, the Nigerian government is able to electrify schools and reduce the burden on the national grid, creating a win-win for both sides.

3. Show Commitment to Local Impact

Governments want to see that your project benefits more than just your bottom line. Demonstrating a commitment to local impact —through job creation, training programs, or social initiatives— builds trust and improves the odds of securing government backing. When your success is their success, everyone's invested in making it work.

- **Example**: d.light, a company providing solar power to communities in Africa and Asia, emphasizes local impact by training local entrepreneurs and creating distribution networks. This commitment to community development has helped d.light build strong relationships with local governments, securing its position in key markets.

Lesson Learned: Government support can be the difference between a sustainable project and a short-lived one. Take advantage of incentives, look for public-private partnership opportunities, and show that you're invested in local impact.

Lessons for Future Renewable Energy Pioneers

Africa's renewable energy revolution is an inspiring story for any entrepreneur looking to make an impact in developing markets. Here's what you can learn from their successes:

1. Think Decentralized for Maximum Reach

Centralized energy grids are often costly and inefficient in developing nations. Decentralized solutions, like solar microgrids, can serve remote areas at a fraction of the cost. When you think outside the grid, you unlock new markets that traditional energy companies simply can't reach.

2. Be Ready to Flex with Regulations

Regulatory landscapes shift, and the most successful companies are the ones that can adapt quickly. Stay agile, keep local experts in your corner, and be ready to pivot when the rules change. A flexible approach will keep you competitive even in the face of new regulations.

3. Build Bridges with Governments and Communities

The best renewable energy projects are partnerships, not solo ventures. Forge alliances with local governments, collaborate with NGOs, and engage community leaders. The more you build goodwill, the smoother your path to growth will be.

Example: Azuri Technologies partners with NGOs and community organizations to bring solar power to rural Africa. By involving community stakeholders, they ensure that their products meet local needs and build trust that drives long-term success.

Final Thoughts on the Renewable Energy Revolution

The renewable energy movement in developing nations is more than just a trend—it's the future. By bringing clean, affordable energy to regions that have long been underserved, renewable startups are changing lives, creating jobs, and setting new standards for sustainable development. If you're considering entering this space, there's no better time to jump in.

Take a page from Africa's playbook: think local, act flexible, and build strong partnerships. Because in the end, this "Green Gold Rush" isn't just about profit; it's about making a lasting, positive impact in places that need it most.

CONCLUSION: BECOMING A GLOBAL GOLD RUSH VISIONARY

Summary of Core Lessons: Revisiting Key Takeaways on Spotting and Capitalizing on International Gold Rush Opportunities

As we've journeyed through the case studies, strategies, and challenges of building a global brand, some essential truths about "Gold Rush" opportunities have emerged. Whether you're eyeing e-commerce in Asia, renewable energy in developing nations, or fintech in Africa, the principles remain the same. Let's revisit the core lessons from our guide:

1. **Start with Market Demand**: Every Gold Rush is fueled by demand—whether it's for better financial access, sustainable energy, or seamless online shopping. To spot these opportunities, keep your finger on the pulse of what people truly need.
2. **Be Ready to Adapt**: Success in global markets requires adaptability. It's not enough to show up with a one-size-fits-all approach. Take the time to understand cultural nuances, local regulations, and consumer preferences in each market.

3. **Forge Strategic Partnerships**: From logistics to payment providers, partnerships are often the secret ingredient in global expansion. Working with local experts allows you to scale faster, reduce risk, and deliver a localized experience.
4. **Embrace Technology**: Technology is the backbone of most successful global ventures. Whether it's AI-driven logistics, mobile payments, or decentralized energy solutions, the right tech enables you to operate efficiently, overcome infrastructure challenges, and serve customers wherever they are.
5. **Create a Long-Term Vision**: Entering a market isn't just about immediate gains. Building a brand that lasts requires a long-term vision, a commitment to quality, and an openness to change. Stay adaptable, stay customer-focused, and always be looking forward.

These lessons aren't just steps in a process; they're principles for building a resilient, successful business on the global stage.

A Call to Action for Aspiring Global Entrepreneurs

If there's one thing to take away from this guide, it's that opportunities are everywhere. But to capture them, you have to look beyond your comfort zone. The world is full of untapped potential, underserved markets, and problems just waiting to be solved. This is your call to action: dare to take your business international. Embrace the unknown, be bold in the face of challenges, and never underestimate the power of a fresh perspective.

There will be bumps in the road, yes, but each obstacle is an opportunity to learn, pivot, and grow. International markets hold endless possibilities, and those willing to take the leap will find themselves at the forefront of the next global Gold Rush. So, gear up, do your homework, and get ready to make your mark on the world. Your adventure in global entrepreneurship starts now.

Final Thoughts on the Future of Global Opportunities

Looking ahead, it's clear that globalization and digital connectivity will continue to reshape the landscape of opportunity. The barriers that once defined "local" versus "global" markets are breaking down, making it easier than ever to connect with customers, partners, and teams worldwide. New technologies like AI, blockchain, and 5G will fuel this shift, creating more efficient supply chains, unlocking access to previously unreachable markets, and making global business possible for even the smallest startups.

But with greater access comes greater competition. The next wave of Gold Rushes will require not just innovation but a deep commitment to understanding and meeting the needs of diverse communities. Those who succeed will be the ones who recognize that global business is as much about connecting with people as it is about creating profit.

The future is wide open, and if you're ready to seize the opportunity, the world is yours to explore. Go forth and discover where the next Gold Rush will take you—and what impact you can make along the way.

APPENDIX

Global Market Research Resources

Entering a new market starts with solid research. Below are some of the best tools, databases, and organizations to help you understand international markets, evaluate demand, and stay on top of economic trends. These resources offer insights into consumer behavior, industry benchmarks, economic forecasts, and regulatory updates—everything you need to make informed decisions.

Recommended Tools & Databases

1. **Statista**: A go-to source for statistics, market reports, and industry insights across dozens of countries and sectors. Statista covers everything from consumer behavior to economic indicators, making it invaluable for global market research.
2. **Euromonitor International**: Known for its in-depth reports on consumer trends and industry insights, Euromonitor's data spans more than 100 countries. It's particularly useful for understanding consumer behavior and demand in emerging markets.
3. **World Bank Open Data**: This free resource provides extensive datasets on global development indicators, including economic growth, infrastructure, education, and more. World Bank data can help you assess economic stability, demographic trends, and potential growth areas in target markets.
4. **NielsenIQ**: For consumer behavior insights, NielsenIQ is a trusted resource. Their data covers FMCG (fast-

moving consumer goods) trends, retail sales, and consumer sentiment in multiple regions.
5. **PwC's Doing Business Guides**: PwC offers guides for setting up businesses in various countries, covering taxes, legal frameworks, and regulatory requirements. These guides are particularly helpful for understanding the essentials of entering a new market.

Organizations and Networks

1. **Export.gov**: The U.S. Department of Commerce's export site provides resources, trade data, and country guides. It's a great place to start for businesses looking to understand regulatory requirements and find local partners.
2. **The International Trade Centre (ITC)**: ITC offers market analysis tools, training programs, and trade information for small and medium enterprises interested in exporting. ITC's market profiles are useful for evaluating trade potential in emerging markets.
3. **Chambers of Commerce**: Many countries have active Chambers of Commerce that support international businesses. The American Chamber of Commerce (AmCham) network, for example, offers insights, networking, and advocacy resources in countries worldwide.
4. **World Economic Forum (WEF)**: WEF's Global Competitiveness Reports provide an overview of economic stability, infrastructure, and innovation across global markets. These reports are useful for identifying strong economic environments and assessing long-term growth prospects.

Cultural Sensitivity Checklist for Entrepreneurs

Understanding cultural differences can make or break your international success. A little knowledge and respect go a long way in building trust and avoiding missteps. Use this checklist to ensure you're interacting thoughtfully and respectfully with diverse audiences.

Language and Communication

- **Use Local Language When Possible**: Even basic greetings or phrases in the local language can show respect and make a good impression.
- **Avoid Jargon**: Be mindful of idioms or expressions that might not translate well.
- **Nonverbal Communication**: Recognize that gestures, eye contact, and personal space expectations vary. Research these norms to avoid unintentional offense.

Social Etiquette

- **Formality**: Start formal in your communication and adjust based on the local culture and cues. Many cultures value formal greetings and titles.
- **Gifting**: In some cultures, small gifts are a common business courtesy; in others, they may be discouraged. Research local customs to determine what's appropriate.
- **Timing**: Punctuality expectations differ widely. In some cultures, being on time is crucial, while others have more flexible attitudes. Understand the standard in your target market.

Business Practices

- **Hierarchy**: In countries where hierarchy is respected, addressing senior team members first shows awareness and respect for local business norms.
- **Decision-Making**: Some cultures prefer consensus-based decisions, while others rely on top-down authority. Tailor your approach based on local preferences.

- **Building Relationships**: Many cultures value building a relationship before jumping into business. Take the time to establish trust and show genuine interest in long-term partnerships.

Religious and Cultural Sensitivities

- **Respect Holidays and Religious Practices**: Be aware of major holidays and local religious practices. Planning meetings and deadlines around these observances shows respect.
- **Dress Code**: Some cultures have specific expectations for business attire. Research local standards and dress accordingly, especially for formal meetings.
- **Be Mindful of Dietary Restrictions**: If hosting a business lunch or dinner, inquire about dietary restrictions to ensure your guests are comfortable.

Business Setup Essentials in Key Markets

Starting a business in a new country can be a maze of paperwork, permits, and fees. Here's a quick reference guide on setup requirements in popular emerging markets like India, Brazil, and Southeast Asia. These essentials will help you anticipate what's needed to get your business off the ground smoothly.

India

- **Business Structures**: Common structures include Private Limited Companies, LLPs (Limited Liability Partnerships), and Sole Proprietorships. Private Limited Companies are the most popular for foreign entities.
- **Registration Process**: You'll need a Digital Signature Certificate (DSC), Director Identification Number (DIN), and a Certificate of Incorporation. The process is overseen by the Ministry of Corporate Affairs.
- **Foreign Direct Investment (FDI)**: India allows 100% FDI in many sectors, but some industries (like media and defense) have FDI caps. Check sector-specific

guidelines to ensure compliance.
- **Taxes**: Companies are subject to corporate income tax, GST (Goods and Services Tax), and import duties. Tax rates vary by industry, so it's wise to consult a local advisor.

Brazil

- **Business Structures**: Foreign companies commonly set up as Limitada (Ltda), similar to an LLC, or Sociedade Anônima (S.A.), similar to a corporation. Limitada is simpler and often preferred.
- **Registration Process**: Businesses must register with the Board of Trade, obtain a CNPJ (business tax ID) from the Receita Federal, and enroll in municipal and state tax programs.
- **Taxes**: Brazil's tax system is complex, with federal, state, and municipal taxes. Corporate income tax, social security contributions, and indirect taxes (like ICMS for goods) are key obligations.
- **Local Representation**: Foreign companies must appoint a local representative, known as a "legal representative," for official documentation.

Southeast Asia (ASEAN Countries)

Each Southeast Asian country has its unique setup requirements, but here are some common essentials:

- **Singapore**: Known for its business-friendly environment, Singapore requires a company to appoint at least one local director, register with ACRA (Accounting and Corporate Regulatory Authority), and pay corporate income tax at a flat rate of 17%.
- **Vietnam**: Foreign companies typically register as Limited Liability Companies (LLCs) or Joint Stock Companies (JSCs). You'll need to register with the Department of Planning and Investment and obtain a Foreign Investment Certificate.
- **Indonesia**: Companies often register as PT PMA (foreign-owned limited liability companies). Registration

with the BKPM (Indonesia Investment Coordinating Board) is required, as well as a tax ID.
- **Thailand**: Most foreign businesses register as Limited Companies. Thailand has a unique Foreign Business License requirement for sectors not fully open to foreign ownership.

Regional Considerations:

- **Local Partnerships**: Many Southeast Asian countries encourage joint ventures with local partners, especially in restricted industries.
- **Investment Incentives**: The ASEAN region frequently offers tax holidays, investment allowances, and duty exemptions for foreign businesses, particularly in tech, manufacturing, and renewable energy.

Final Note: Regulations in each country can change frequently, and additional requirements may apply based on your industry. Always consult a local expert to ensure compliance with the latest rules.

www.ingramcontent.com/pod-product-compliance
Lightning Source LLC
Chambersburg PA
CBHW070153230526
45471CB00002B/642